ESSENTIAL INSTANT POT COOKBOOK For Beginners

Easy & Most Foolproof Instant Pot Recipes Cookbook for Everyday Cooking And your Instant Pot

BY

Clara Michael

ISBN: 978-1-952504-57-0

COPYRIGHT © 2020 by Clara Michael

All rights reserved. This book is copyright protected and it's for personal use only. Without the prior written permission of the publisher, no part of this publication should be reproduced, distributed, or transmitted in any form or by any means, including photocopying, recording, or other electronic or mechanical methods.

This publication is sold with the idea that the publisher is not required to render accounting, officially permitted, or otherwise, qualified services. Seek for the services of a legal or professional, a practiced individual in the profession if advice is needed.

DISCLAIMER

The information contained in this book is geared for educational and entertainment purposes only. Concerted efforts have been made towards providing accurate, up to date and reliable complete information. The information in this book is true and complete to the best of our knowledge.

Neither the publisher nor the author takes any responsibility for any possible consequences of reading or enjoying the recipes in this book. The author and publisher disclaim any liability in connection with the use of information contained in this book. Under no circumstance will any legal responsibility or blame be apportioned against the author or publisher for any reparation, damages, or monetary loss due to the information herein, either directly or indirectly.

Table of Contents

INTRODUCTION 8

What is Instant Pot? 8

Reasons Why You Need an Instant Pot 9

Making Sense of Those Buttons 11

Step-by-Step Guide to Clean Your Instant Pot Effectively 14

INSTANT POT BREAKFAST RECIPES 16

    Breakfast Cobbler 16

    Pumpkin Spice Latte Oats 17

    Crustless Tomato Spinach Quiche 18

    Berries and Cream Breakfast Cake 19

    Mushroom Risotto 21

    Hidden Cauliflower Mac 'n' Cheese 22

    Breakfast Burritos 23

    BrothyFarro with Sausage and Leeks 24

    Vanilla latte Steel Cut Oats 26

    Macaroni and Cheese 27

    Buckwheat Porridge 28

    Caldo Verde 29

    Brown Butter Steel-Cut Oatmeal 30

INSTANT POT SOUP & STEW RECIPES 31

    Vietnamese Chicken Noodle Soup 31

    Italian Beef Stew 33

    Vegetable Soup 34

    Italian Sausage Stew 35

    Cheddar Broccoli and Potato Soup 37

    Spanish Infused Chicken Stew 38

Chicken Noodle Soup 39

Tomato Chick Pea Soup 40

Irish Stew 42

Creamy Thai Coconut Chicken Soup 44

Smoky Lentil and Potato Soup 45

INSTANT POT FISH & SEAFOOD RECIPES 46

Shrimp Scampi 46

Steamed Alaskan Crab Legs 47

10-Minute Instant Pot Salmon 48

Shrimp Paella 49

Coconut Fish Curry 51

Chipotle Shrimp Soup 53

Cajun Shrimp and Sausage Boil 55

Lemon Pepper Salmon 57

Crustless Crab Quiche 58

Lobster Bisque 60

INSTANT POT POULTRY RECIPES 61

Teriyaki Chicken & Rice 61

Salsa Lime Chicken 62

Chicken Adobo 63

Buffalo Chicken Soup with Crumbled Blue Cheese 64

Honey Garlic Chicken 66

Mongolian Chicken 67

Creamy Italian Chicken Breasts 69

Chicken Marsala 70

Chicken Cacciatore 71

Chicken Cordon Bleu 72

    Chicken Chile Verde 73

INSTANT POT BEAN & GRAIN RECIPES 74

    Refried Black Beans 74

    Spiced Coconut Chicken and Rice 75

    Mexican Rice and Beans 77

    New Orleans-Style Red Beans and Rice 78

    Red Beans and Rice with Sausage 80

    Cherry & Spice Rice Pudding 82

    Beans and Brown Rice 83

INSTANT POT LAMB, BEEF & PORK RECIPES 85

    Beef and Butternut Squash Stew 85

    Boneless Pork Chops 87

    Sticky Hoisin Baby Back Ribs 88

    Japanese Pork Tender Rib Stew 89

    BBQ Baby Back Ribs ....**Error! Bookmark not defined.**

    Cuban Pulled Pork Sandwiches 92

    Pork Vindaloo 94

    Korean Beef 96

    Mini Meatballs with Radiatori 97

    Pork Chops 98

    Lamb Stew 99

    Hearty Beef Stew 100

INSTANT POT EGG RECIPES 101

    Poached Eggs 101

    Bacon Cheddar Egg Casserole 102

    Eggy Muffins 103

    Sous Vide Egg Bites 104

Sriracha and Red Pepper Deviled Eggs 105

Egg Pudding 106

Cheesy Egg Bake 107

Chinese Savory Steamed Egg 108

Hard Boiled Eggs 109

Quick Egg Custard 110

French "Baked" Eggs 111

Artichoke and Asparagus Deviled Eggs 112

INSTANT POT VEGAN RECIPES 113

Vegan Cauliflower Queso 113

Lentil Curry 115

Vegan Potato Curry 116

Vegan Lentil Chili 117

Easy Jackfruit Curry 118

Maple Bourbon Sweet Potato Chili 120

Green Chile Stew 122

Easy Vegan Mashed Potatoes 124

Vegan Butter Chicken 126

INSTANT POT APPETIZER RECIPES 128

Homemade Peaches and Cream Oatmeal 128

Cocktail Meatballs 129

Buffalo Ranch Chicken Dip 130

Beer-Braised Pulled Ham 131

Cranberry Pecan Brie 132

Prosciutto-wrapped Asparagus Canes 133

Chicken Tikka Bites 134

Cheddar Bacon Ale Dip 135

Hoisin Meatballs 136

Hearty Pork & Black Bean Nachos 137

INSTANT POT DESSERT RECIPES 139

Blueberry Cornmeal Breakfast Cake 139

Apple Bread with Salted Caramel Icing 140

Chunky Apple Cake 141

Apple Crisp 142

Molten Mocha Cake 143

Mason Jar Steel Cut Oats 144

Vanilla Cheesecake 145

INTRODUCTION

What is Instant Pot?

The Instant Pot is an electronic cooking device or machine programmed to perform the function of 7 gadgets. Unlike electric pressure cooker, steamer, slow cooker, yoghurt maker, rice cooker, warming pot or sauté pan, Instant Pot is a cooker programmed with multi-functions which can perform the same task like the afore mentioned machines. The Instant Pot is a seven-in-one multi cooker combined that can work as an electric pressure cooker, steamer, slow cooker, yoghurt maker, rice cooker, and sauté pan. It can cook meals instantly and faster but it has an option for a start time that can be programmed to delay.

Some people that likes convenient cooking and the option of "set it and forget it" in a slow cooker would have a great passion for Instant Pot and also including those who desires to have a pressure cooker, steamer, yoghurt maker and slow cooker simultaneously but has little or no space to occupy the four cookers, Instant Pot performs the same functions like the other four machines. The Instant Pot comes with instruction manual and short booklet of recipes which contain functions of Instant Pot and manufacturer's recommended quantities of food ingredients together with preparation and cooking times to help the newbies.

The Instant Pot will save you a whole lots of time if you wants to cook food like stew, lentils or grains. The special thing about Instant Pot is that it has a lot of functional uses for a single appliance and you can set it and walk away doing other things while the machine does its magic. With its multi-functional ability, it may seem difficult to operate your Instant Pot but it's very easy to operate when you follow the instruction manual.

Reasons Why You Need an Instant Pot

1. **It Can Cook Beans Super-Fast.**

This reason alone got my attention to this fabulous Instant Pot device. While it takes some people about 12-15 minutes to cook soaked beans and 37-40 minutes to cook dry beans. I was not fully convinced when the Instant Pot cook beans very fast until I heard it over and over again from different people and their good comments made about their Instant Pot. That was when I started having great passion for Instant Pot and it earned a space in my kitchen.

2. **To Make Perfect Brown Rice.**

It's not easy to cook brown rice but it was easy for me. I have been thinking brown rice was easy to cook but was doubtful the first time I cooked brown rice with little water and I thought I would made crunchy rice. However, the rice was not crunchy as I thought and it was perfect rice I have ever cooked. You can use your Instant Pot to make recipes like Mexican Casserole, Cheesy Broccoli and Rice Casserole perfectly in a fraction of the time.

3. **Steam/Cook Veggies in Minutes.**

The Instant Pot cooks veggies in minutes. When cooking veggies, do not walk away to avoid burning or overcooking your veggies. It's important to stick to the step by step recipes instructions when cooking veggies. I've burned more than my fair share of veggies by forgetting about them. You have to make use of quick pressure release to release the steam once they are finished cooking.

4. **Built in Timer.**

What amazes me the most about the Instant Pot machine is the fact that you can cook a meal, walk away and come back later to meet fully cooked meals. The Instant Pot will not start cooking by itself until you want it to cook by using the timer. You can program your dinner to start at 4:30pm and keep it warm until you get home.

5. **Easy Clean Up.**

Washing of my dishes is one of the things I have little time to do. I do avoid cooking dishes that will require thorough washing of dishes. When it comes to Instant Pot, it is very easy to clean up after use.

6. **Pressure Cooking Retains More Nutrients.**

Researchers have it that food cooked for a short time with less water retains more nutrients. Instant Pot retains more nutrients because of its short duration used for cooking. Due to the high pressure, beans and grains become more digestible.

7. **They are Safe.**

There are some reports on injuries or dangers of pressure cookers blowing up while cooking. Some people became scared of using pressure cooker because of some domestic violence caused by the pressure cooker. However, Instant Pot is very safe to use. It has 10 in-built safety features which include high temperature warning, a lid which is to be locked while cooking, automatic pressure control and many others.

8. **Slow Cooker.**

The Instant Pot is a little taller but has the same size with slow cookers. The Instant Pot also perform the function of a slow cooker by just pressing a button. Some people may decide to use their Instant Pot as a slow cooker on regular bases. By doing this, you must make sure you buy the optional lid so you can be able to use the Instant Pot as a slow cooker on regular basis.

9. **Sauté feature.**

The Instant Pot has a sauté feature. It means the Instant Pot can also perform the function of a sauté pan. So you can toss onions and garlic in, select sauté button, prepare the rest of your ingredients and then add them to the pot and set the time you want Instant Pot to cook whatever you wants to cook.

Making Sense of Those Buttons

1. **Manual / Pressure Buttons:**

   This function will be frequently used which enables you to select the cooking time manually and pressure cook what you wants to cook. The Instant Pot pressure, time and temperature can be adjusted by pressing the "+/-" features. It is imperative to follow the recipe instructions to know if you are to pressure cook the food using Low or High Pressure. The "Manual" and "Pressure" button stands for pressure cooking unlike functions like "Sauté", "Yogurt" or "Slow cooker" which does not require pressure cooking. The Instant Pot's default setting is High Pressure when you press the "Manual" button.

2. **Sauté Button:**

   This feature is the second most frequently used button on the Instant Pot. You can select the sauté button to cook up anything as you would in a skillet or pan without 1 cup of liquid. All you need to do is just to set the "Sauté" button, add some cooking oil like butter, avocado, coconut or animal fat like beef tallow or lard to the inner pot and add food you want to cook like a skillet or pan. The sauté button can be used to cook ingredients like onion, garlic and meat. Most times, I start with the "Sauté" function and then use the "Manual" / "Pressure" button to pressure cook my meal.

3. **Slow Cook Button:**

   This button helps you to use Instant Pot like a slower cooker. This function allows the Instant Pot to perform the function of a slow cooker. Just add food as you normally do to a slow cooker, secure the lid and then select the "Slow Cook" button and use "+/-" buttons to adjust the cook time.

4. **Bean / Chili:**

   This button allows the Instant Pot to cook beans faster than any other cooker. This is why beans is the food I like cooking most in my Instant Pot. The "Bean / Chili" button, uses the default High Pressure for 30 minutes though it can be adjusted for "More" to High Pressure for 35 minutes or "Less" for High Pressure for 20 minutes. Black beans take about 10-15 minutes, while kidney beans take 20-25. The Instant Pot Manual has different cooking times for various beans and legumes.

5. **Meat / Stew:**

   The Instant Pot can easily make your favorite stew or meat dish. It can make it by adjusting the settings depending on the desired texture. For instance, a homemade stew with about 1-2 lb. of meat, you can set it to "Meat / Stew" button using high pressure for 35 minutes. The "More" setting is great for fall-off-the-bone cooking. It will set to a default High Pressure for 35 minutes. The Instant Pot can be adjusted for "More" to High Pressure for 45 minutes or "Less" for High Pressure for 20 minutes.

6. **Multigrain:**

This function can be used for cooking wild rice or brown rice which usually takes longer time than cooking white rice. Cook brown rice to a 1:1.25 ratio rice to water and wild rice to a 1:3 ratio rice to water for 25-30 minutes. The default (Normal) setting is 40 minutes of cooking time but can be adjusted as required for the "Less" setting to 20 minutes of cooking time, or "More" at 45 minutes of warm water soaking and 60 minutes of cooking.

7. **Porridge:**

Rice porridge (congee) and other grains can be cooked using the porridge button.

The default cooking time on High Pressure for rice porridge is 20 minutes but can be adjusted for "More" to High Pressure for 30 minutes or "Less" for High Pressure for 15 minutes. When the cooking cycle has completed, it is not advisable to use Quick Pressure Release because it has high starch content and may splatter the porridge through the steam release vent. It's imperative to use the Natural Pressure Release to release the steam.

8. **Poultry:**

This button can be used for making chicken and other poultry recipes in the Instant Pot. The default cooking program is 15 minutes but can be adjusted for "More" to High Pressure for 30 minutes or "Less" for High Pressure for 5 minutes. I always make shredded chicken for homemade tacos and burrito bowls. Add about 1 lb. uncooked chicken, ¼ cup of homemade salsa, 1 cup of bone broth, 1 tsp. cumin, 1 clove garlic minced, ½ tsp oregano, ½ onion, and $^{1/8}$ tsp. paprika into the bottom of your Instant Pot. Secure the lid in place and select the "Poultry" button to the default at High Pressure for 15 minutes. When the cooking cycle has finished, do a Natural Pressure Release for 10 minutes. Carefully open the lid, shred the chicken the two forks, add pepper and salt to taste.

9. **Rice:**

This button is used to cook rice in your Instant Pot using half the time a conventional rice cooker could use. It uses about 4 to 8 minutes, short grain, Jasmine, White rice, and Basmati rice can all be cooked using this function. You'll need a 1:1 ratio of rice to water (Basmati is a 1:1.5 ratio). It depends on the quantity of food you want to cook on low pressure, when you press the "Rice" button, the cooking duration automatically adjusts. It's always necessary to add further 10-12 minutes to the cooking time to allow the Instant Pot to come to pressure but cooking rice in the "Manual" mode at high pressure is my frequent selection. I usually add 1:1 ratio of rice to water into the bottom of my Instant Pot and set to 3 minutes with a 12 minute Natural Pressure Release when the timer beeps..

10. **Soup:**

Soup, stock, and broth can be made using the "Soup" button. Water doesn't heavily boil because Instant Pot will control the pressure and temperature so that the liquid doesn't heavily boil. You can adjust the cooking time as required, usually between 20-40 minutes, and the pressure to either Low or High Pressure. Anytime you wish to make homemade bone broth faster than the conventional slow cooker, it is very simple. Click the "Soup" button, set the Low Pressure, and set the cooking time to 120 minutes. Once the timer beeps, do Natural Pressure Release to release the steam.

11. **Steam:**

This button can be used to steam vegetables, seafood or reheat food. Always use the steam rack of your Instant Pot when steaming veggies to avoid burning and sticking to the bottom of your Instant Pot. Add 1-2 cups of water to the inner liner, place the steam rack inside the inner pot and with a stainless steel steam basket on top. Add the vegetables, seafood, etc. in the basket. Select the "Steam" button and then adjust the time using the "+" or "-" key. When you are cooking foods like frozen corn on the cob or a fresh fish filet, adjust the time to 3-5 minutes and 8-10 minutes if you are cooking fresh artichokes could take 9-11 minutes.

12. **Keep Warm Button:**

This button is used to keep food hot when the Instant Pot is done with cooking or to cancel the pressure cooking mode. Immediately cooking time is finished, the Instant Pot will beep and automatically go into the "Keep Warm" function. It will display an "L" in front of a number to indicate how long it's been warm – e.g. "L0:30" for 30 minutes. This button helps to keep food warm (145 to 172°F) for up to 99 hours, 50 minutes.

13. **Cancel Button:**

If by mistake you selected wrong cooking time and you want to stop cooking or adjust pressure cooking time, you can cancel and return to standby mode by selecting the "Keep Warm" / "Cancel" button.

14. **Timer Button**

This button can be used to delay the cooking start time for the Instant Pot for both pressure cooking and slow cook options. Press the Timer button with 10 seconds of pressing Pressure / Manual button or Slow Cook button. To adjust the delayed hours, Use "+/-" buttons then wait a second and press Timer again to set delayed minutes. Press the Keep Warm / Cancel button to cancel the Timer anytime

Step-by-Step Guide to Clean Your Instant Pot Effectively

Step 1: Unplug

Before you start cleaning your Instant Pot, make sure it is unplugged. It's advisable to unplug your Instant Pot whenever it's not in use. For this purpose, you have to make sure it's unplugged for the intensive cleaning you're about to do, for the safety of your Instant Pot and for your safety too.

Step 2: Cleaning housing unit

The outside housing unit cannot go into the dishwasher so you should be able to clean it thoroughly with a rag. Get the rag good and damp with water and cleaning solution, and wipe down both the interior and exterior parts of the main housing unit. To have a perfect cleaning, a sponge is recommended to get those hard or stiff food bits and mineral deposits. Don't fail to clean everywhere you may have tiny particles.

Step 3: Wash the lid

The lid has to be washed properly. This can be done by washing it in the sink with warm water with a little dish soap to make all the residuals are removed because this can contaminate. Some people used a vinegar solution to remove the unpleasant smell from residuals.

Step 4: Check other crevices

There are some parts in the Instant Pot that you might not like to cleaning all the time you are washing the Instant Pot. Get all those crevices and small parts where food residue may build up for some period of time. Remove the Quick Release handle, and wash it with warm-soapy water. In some cases, the steam valve can get blocked if too much deposit builds up there. Remove the shield, located inside the lid which blocks the valve. The shield could pop off easily depending on the model your Instant Pot. Wash the shield in the sink. Check the condensation collection cup at the side of your Instant Pot. It might have collected food residue over time. If it has some residue on it, clean it in the sink.

Step 5: clean sealing ring

The silicone ring found on the underside of the lid will likely need a thorough cleaning. This is what indicates your Instant Pot has a tight seal, and it's an easy spot for food particles or residual smells to lurk. Check it for any signs of damage, as silicone can start to crack over time. If you notice any crack in the silicone ring, it has been damaged and needs a replacement immediately. The silicone ring is dishwasher-safe, so you can pop it in there on the top rack. Once it's thoroughly cleaned, place it back on the underside of the lid, and make sure you've got a secure fit.

Step 6: Wash the inner pot

The inner pot is dishwasher-safe. With this fact, you should be washing the inner pot at regularly intervals. Since you're doing a deep clean, it doesn't hurt to pop the inner pot into the dishwasher together with any of the other dishwasher-safe parts you use with your Instant Pot, such as silicone molds and wire racks. When you finished washing the inner pot, dry it off using a paper towel or use some household vinegar to give it a thorough wipe-down. By doing this, it can get rid of any accumulated residue from things like minerals in your water, or dish detergent. This will make your Instant Pot looks shiny and nice.

Step 7: Steam clean and let dry

At this stage, you have done a thorough cleaning, reassemble all the parts. Don't forget about those small parts like the sealing ring and shield because they can be missed easily. The purpose of this washing and cleaning is to ensure your Instant Pot is safe so you can use it for a long period of time. However, after doing all the washing and cleaning but you realized the sealing ring still has a strange food smell, you may need to deodorize the part with a vinegar steam clean. The process is simple and can be done directly in the Instant Pot by adding a cup of water, a cup of vinegar, and some lemon peels (for extra freshness!) to the inner pot, press "Steam" button and set for a few minutes. When the timer beeps, do a natural pressure release. Open the lid, remove the sealing ring and dry it at a convenient place.

INSTANT POT BREAKFAST RECIPES

Breakfast Cobbler

Preparation time: 10 minutes

Cook time: 15minutes

Total time: 25 minutes

Serves: 3

Ingredients:

- 1 Pear, diced
- 1 Apple, diced
- 1 Plum, diced
- 2 Tbsp. (30 ml) local honey
- 3 Tbsp. (45 ml) coconut oil
- 1/4 Tsp. ground cinnamon
- 1/4 Cup of unsweetened shredded coconut
- 1/4 (30 g) Cup of pecan pieces
- 2 Tbsp. (20 g) sunflower seeds (salted and roasted will work)

Optional garnish: Coconut whipped cream

Cooking Instructions:

1. Add your cut fruit into the stainless steel bowl of your Instant Pot.

2. Spoon in the honey and coconut oil, sprinkle the cinnamon, secure the lid and lock the pressure valve.

3. Press the Steam button and allow the fruit to cook for about 12 minutes. Quick release the pressure when the cooking time is up.

4. Remove the lid and turn the cooked fruit with a slotted spoon or skimmer into a serving bowl.

5. Keep the coconut, pecans, and sunflower seeds into the residual liquid and press the Sauté button.

6. Allow the contents to cook for about 6minutes, shifting them regularly so they do not burn. When they are nicely browned and toasted, remove them and top your cooked fruit.

7. Serve immediately and enjoy!

Pumpkin Spice Latte Oats

Preparation time: 8 minutes

Cook time: 23 minutes

Total time: 31 minutes

Serves: 5

Ingredients:

- 1 Cup of steel cut oats
- 2 Cups of water
- 1 Cup milk
- 1/2 Cup of pumpkin puree
- 1 Tsp. pumpkin pie spice
- Pinch of salt
- Pinch of black pepper
- 1/4 Cup of brown sugar
- 2 Tbsp. of vanilla
- 1/2 Cup of strong coffee
- 1/4 Cup of half and half or heavy cream

Cooking Instructions:

1. Mix oats, water, and milk in your Instant Pot.

2. Select Manual High Pressure to cook for about 23 minutes.

3. When timer beeps, use natural pressure release for about 5 minutes, then release any remaining pressure.

4. Stir in pumpkin, pumpkin pie spice, salt, pepper, brown sugar, vanilla, and coffee.

5. Flip into a serving bowl or mug, top with some extra brown sugar and a drizzle of heavy cream.

6. Serve and enjoy!

Crustless Tomato Spinach Quiche

Preparation time: 10 minutes

Cook time: 15 minutes

Total time: 25 minutes

Serves: 7

Ingredients:

- 12 Large eggs
- 1 Cup of milk
- ½ Tsp. salt
- ¼ Tsp. fresh ground black pepper
- 3 Cups of fresh baby spinach, roughly chopped
- 1 Cup of diced seeded tomato
- 4 Large green onions, sliced
- 4 Tomato slices for topping the quiche
- ½ Cup of shredded Parmesan cheese

Cooking Instructions:

1. Place a trivet in the bottom of the Instant Pot and add 1 ½ cups of water.

2. Whisk together the eggs, milk, salt and pepper in a large bowl. Add the spinach, tomato, and green onions to a 1 ½ quart baking dish and mix well.

3. Pour egg mixture over the veggies and stir to combine and carefully place sliced tomatoes on top and sprinkle with Parmesan cheese.

4. Use a sling to place the dish on the trivet in the pressure cooking pot and Close the lid in place. Select Manual High Pressure to cook for about 15 minutes.

5. When timer beeps, use natural pressure release for about 7 minutes, then release any remaining pressure.

6. Open the lid, lift out the dish and if desired, broil until lightly browned.

7. Serve and enjoy!

Berries and Cream Breakfast Cake

Preparation time: 8 minutes

Cook time: 10 minutes

Total time: 18 minutes

Serves: 6

Ingredients:

Breakfast Cake:

- 5 Eggs
- ¼ Cup of sugar
- 2 Tbsp. butter, melted
- ¾ Cup of ricotta cheese
- ¾ Cup of plain or vanilla yogurt
- 2 Tsp. vanilla extract
- 1 Cup of whole wheat pastry flour or white whole wheat flour
- ½ Tsp. salt
- 2 Tsp. baking powder
- ½ Cup of Berry Compote
- Berry Compote (prepare and chill beforehand)

Sweet Yogurt Glaze:

- ¼ Cup of yogurt
- ½ Tsp. vanilla extract
- 1 Tsp. milk
- 1-2 Tbsp. powdered sugar

Cooking Instructions:

1. Prepare the Berry Compote beforehand so it is cold and thick. It has a tendency to sink to the bottom of the pan if used warmed.

2. For the Breakfast Cake, carefully grease a 6 cup Bundt pan with nonstick cooking spray.

3. Beat together the eggs and sugar until smooth. Add the butter, ricotta cheese, yogurt, and vanilla and mix until smooth.

4. Using a separate bowl, whisk together the flour, salt, and baking powder. Combine with the egg mixture. Pour into the prepared Bundt pan.

5. Using ½ cup of Berry Compote, sprinkle on top of the batter and swirl in with a knife.

6. Add 1 cup of water to the Instant Pot and place a trivet inside. Carefully place the Bundt pan on the trivet.

7. Cover the lid and turn pressure release knob to a sealed position. Cook at High Pressure for 25 minutes.

8. While the cake is cooking, make the Sweet Yogurt Glaze by whisking together the yogurt, vanilla, milk, and powdered sugar; set aside.

9. When cooking time is completed, use natural pressure release for 5 minutes and then release any remaining pressure.

10. Remove pan from Instant Pot and allow it to cool for sometimes. Loosen the sides of the cake from the pan and flip onto a serving plate.

11. Serve immediately and enjoy!

Mushroom Risotto

Preparation time: 10 minutes

Cook time: 35 minutes

Total time: 45 minutes

Serves: 7 cups

Ingredients:

- 2 Tbsp. extra-virgin olive oil
- 1 lb. wild mushrooms, trimmed, sliced
- Kosher salt, freshly ground pepper
- 1 Medium onion, chopped
- 2 Cups of Carnaroli or Arborio rice
- 1 Cup of white wine
- 4 Cups of vegetable or chicken stock
- Chopped parsley and finely grated Parmesan (for serving)

Cooking Instructions:

1. Set Instant Pot on medium heat or "Sauté" and pour oil into cooker insert.

2. Add mushrooms and cook about 10 minutes until any moisture they have released is evaporated and they start to brown, season with salt and pepper.

3. Add onion, stir to combine, and cook for about 8 minutes or until translucent. Add rice and stir until chalky white, about 3 minutes.

4. Add wine and cook until mostly evaporated, about 3 minutes. Stir in stock. Close the lid, making sure steam-release valve is in the proper sealed position.

5. Select Manual High Pressure to cook for about 35 minutes. When timer beeps, use natural pressure release for about 10 minutes, then release any remaining pressure.

6. Open the lid. Stir with a wooden spoon; season with salt and pepper. Flip risotto onto serving plates. Top with parsley and Parmesan.

7. Serve and enjoy!

Hidden Cauliflower Mac 'n' Cheese

Preparation time: 5 minutes

Cook time: 5 minutes

Total time: 10 minutes

Serves: 5

Ingredients:

- 1 lb. whole-wheat macaroni
- 4 Cups of water
- 2 Tbsp. soy sauce or tamari
- 1 Tbsp. spicy brown mustard
- 1 ½ Tsp. fine sea salt
- 1 lb. Fresh or frozen cauliflower florets
- 4 oz. Extra-sharp Cheddar
- ¼ Cup of grated Parmesan cheese, or other cheese of your choice, like gruyere

Cooking Instructions:

1. Pour the pasta into the Instant Pot and add the water, soy sauce, mustard, and salt. Stir well to combine.

2. Add the cauliflower on top without stirring, making sure that the cauliflower layer completely covers the pasta for even cooking.

3. Cover the lid and move the steam release valve to sealing position. Select Manual High Pressure to cook for about 5 minutes.

4. When timer beeps, use natural pressure release for about 5 minutes, then release any remaining pressure.

5. Open the lid and stir the pasta well, using a spatula to break up any pasta that has stuck together or stuck to the bottom of the pot.

6. Use the spatula to mash any intact cauliflower florets against the side of the Instant Pot to help them dissolve into the pasta sauce.

7. Add the Cheddar and parmesan and stir well. Taste and adjust the seasonings as needed and flip onto serving plates.

8. Serve and enjoy!

Breakfast Burritos

Preparation time: 10 minutes

Cook time: 25 minutes

Total time: 35 minutes

Serves: 5

Ingredients:

- 2 ½ Cups of O'Brien hash browns
- 1 Cup of diced ham (or protein of your choice)
- 7 Eggs
- ¼ Cup of milk
- ¼ Cup of sour cream
- 1 Cup of shredded cheese
- ¼ Tsp. salt
- 1/8 Tsp pepper

Cooking Instructions:

1. Spray the inner liner with non-stick spray. Measure out and dump the hash browns into the bottom of the liner.

2. Pour the ham (or protein of your choice) on top of the frozen hash browns.

3. In a medium bowl, whisk together the eggs, milk, sour cream shredded cheese, salt and pepper.

4. Pour the eggs into the small liner on top of the hash browns and protein. Cover tightly with foil.

5. In the large liner, pour one cup of water into the bottom and then place the trivet inside of the liner. Place the small 'inner pot' inside of the large pot, onto the trivet.

6. Select Manual High Pressure to cook for about 5 minutes. When timer beeps, use natural pressure release for about 5 minutes, then release any remaining pressure.

7. Carefully take foil off, stir and then replace the foil. Cook a second time on Manual High Pressure for 10 minutes. Flip into tortillas.

8. Serve and enjoy!

BrothyFarro with Sausage and Leeks

Preparation time: 10 minutes

Cook time: 30 minutes

Total time: 40 minutes

Serves: 4

Ingredients:

- 4 Large or 6 small leeks, white and pale-greens parts only
- 1 Tbsp. extra-virgin olive oil, plus more for drizzling
- 4 Fully cooked spicy Italian sausage links (about 12 oz.), sliced crosswise into 1/3"-Thick rounds
- 1 Large bunch scallions (about 10)
- ¼ Cup of dry white wine
- 1 Cup of Offarro
- 1/2 Tsp. kosher salt
- 1/2 Tsp. freshly ground black pepper
- 4 Sprigs thyme
- Thinly sliced radishes, peperoncini, and lemon wedges (for serving)

Cooking Instructions:

1. Preheat Instant Pot on "Sauté" setting.

2. Trim roots off leeks and remove and discard tough outer layers, then cut leeks into 1/3"-thick rounds. Rinse well, then pat dry.

3. When Instant Pot is hot, pour 1 Tbsp. oil into insert. Add sausage and cook, stirring occasionally until browned in places, about 5 minutes.

4. Separate white and light green parts of scallions from dark green parts. Cut white and light green parts into 1/4"-thick rounds.

5. Finely chop dark green parts and set aside. Add leeks and scallion white and light green parts to pressure cooker and stir to coat in oil.

6. Add wine and cook, stirring occasionally, until wine is reduced by half and no longer smells like alcohol, about 1 minute.

7. Add the offarro, salt, pepper, thyme, and 2 ½ cups of water and stir to combine, then turn off cooker.

8. Lock the lid, making sure steam-release valve is in the proper sealed position. Select Manual High Pressure to cook for about 5 minutes.

9. When timer beeps, use natural pressure release for about 5 minutes, then release any remaining pressure. Flip onto serving plates.

10. Top with radishes, pepperoncini, and reserved scallion greens. Drizzle with oil and squeeze lemons over.

11. Serve and enjoy!

Vanilla latte Steel Cut Oats

Preparation time: 10 minutes

Cook time: 30 minutes

Total time: 40 minutes

Serves: 4

Ingredients:

- 2 Cups of water
- 1 Cup of milk
- 1 Cup of steel cut oats
- 2 Tbsp. sugar
- 1 Tsp. espresso powder
- ¼ Tsp salt
- 2 Tsp vanilla extract
- Freshly whipped cream
- Finely grated chocolate

Cooking Instructions:

1. Add water, milk, oats, sugar, espresso powder, and salt to pressure cooking pot.

2. Give everything a good stir to dissolve espresso powder. Lock the lid in place and select Manual High Pressure to cook for 10 minutes.

3. When timer beeps, use natural pressure release for about 5 minutes, then release any remaining pressure.

4. When valve drops carefully remove lid. Stir vanilla extract and additional sugar to taste.

5. Cover and let sit five minutes until oats are desired thickness. Flip onto serving plates.

6. Serve topped with whipped cream and grated chocolate.

Macaroni and Cheese

Preparation time: 5 minutes

Cook time: 6 minutes

Total time: 11 minutes

Serves: 8

Ingredients:

- 1 Lb. elbow macaroni
- 4 Cups of low-sodium chicken broth or vegetable broth
- 3 Tbsp. unsalted butter
- 12 Oz. shredded sharp Cheddar cheese (3 cups tightly packed)
- 1 Cup of shredded Parmesan cheese (about 2 ounces)
- 1 Cup of sour cream
- 2 Tsp. prepared yellow mustard
- 2 Tsp. cayenne pepper

Cooking Instructions:

1. Combine the macaroni, broth, and butter in the Instant Pot.

2. Lock the lid and set the pressure release to sealing position. Select the Manual high pressure setting to cook for 6 minutes.

3. When timer beeps, use natural pressure release for about 5 minutes, then release any remaining pressure.

4. Open the Instant Pot and stir in the cheeses, sour cream, mustard, and cayenne pepper. Let sit for 5 minutes to thicken, and then stir again.

5. Serve and enjoy!

Buckwheat Porridge

Preparation time: 7 minutes

Cook time: 20 minutes

Total time: 27 minutes

Serves: 5

Ingredients:

- 1 Cup of raw buckwheat groats
- 3 Cups of rice milk
- 1 Banana sliced
- ¼ Cup of raisins
- 1 Tsp. ground cinnamon
- ½ Tsp. vanilla
- Chopped nuts optional

Cooking Instructions:

1. Rinse buckwheat and place in Instant Pot.

2. Add rice milk, banana, raisins, cinnamon and vanilla and close lid. Be sure the steam release is in the closed position.

3. Select the Manual high pressure setting to cook for 6 minutes.

4. When timer beeps, use natural pressure release for about 15 minutes, then release any remaining pressure.

5. Once pressure is released, open the lid and stir porridge with a long handled spoon.

6. Add more rice milk to individual servings to achieve preferred consistency. Sprinkle with chopped nuts if desired.

7. Serve and enjoy!

Caldo Verde

Preparation time: 10 minutes

Cook time: 20 minutes

Total time: 30 minutes

Serves: 6

Ingredients:

- 1 ½ Cup of extra-virgin olive oil
- 12 Oz. dry-cured Spanish chorizo or linguiça, casing removed, sliced into 1/4" rounds
- 1 Bunch curly kale, stems removed and thinly sliced, leaves torn into bite-size pieces
- 2 Lb. Yukon Gold potatoes, cut into 1" pieces
- 1 Onion, chopped
- 2 Garlic cloves, chopped
- 1 Tsp. (or more) kosher salt
- ¼ Tsp. freshly ground black pepper
- 2 Bay leaves

Cooking Instructions:

1. Pour oil into Instant Pot and select "Sauté."
2. When it's hot, add sausage and cook for about 5 minutes, stirring occasionally until browned.
3. Pour off excess fat, add kale, potatoes, onion, and garlic, and stir to coat.
4. Season with salt and pepper and add bay leaves and 6 cups water. Stir to combine.
5. Lock on lid, making sure steam release valve is in the proper sealed position.
6. Select the Manual high pressure button to cook for 6 minutes.
7. When timer beeps, use natural pressure release for about 15 minutes, then release any remaining pressure.
8. Taste and add more salt, if needed. Flip onto serving plates.
9. Serve and enjoy!

Brown Butter Steel-Cut Oatmeal

Preparation time: 10 minutes

Cook time: 12 minutes

Total time: 22 minutes

Serves: 4

Ingredients:

- 2 Tbsp. unsalted butter
- 1 ½ Cups of steel-cut oats
- 4 ½ Cups of water
- ½ Tsp. kosher salt

Toppings: Brown sugar and heavy cream

Cooking Instructions:

1. Select Sauté on the Instant Pot and melt the butter.
2. Add the oats and sauté, stirring often, for about 5 minutes or until lightly toasted.
3. Add the water and salt and stir to combine, making sure all of the oats are submerged in the liquid.
4. Secure the lid and set the Pressure Release to sealing position. Select the Porridge setting and set the cooking time for 12 minutes at high pressure.
5. When timer beeps, use natural pressure release for about 10 minutes, then release any remaining pressure.
6. Open the Instant Pot and stir the oatmeal to incorporate any extra liquid. Flip the oatmeal into bowls and top with brown sugar and cream.
7. Serve and enjoy!

INSTANT POT SOUP & STEW RECIPES

Vietnamese Chicken Noodle Soup

Preparation time: 10 minutes

Cook time: 35 minutes

Total time: 45 minutes

Serves: 5

Ingredients:

- 2 Tbsp. canola oil
- 2 Medium yellow onions, halved
- 1 (2-inch) Piece ginger, cut into ¼ -inch slices
- 1 Tbsp. coriander seeds
- 3 Star anise pods
- 5 Cloves
- 1 Cinnamon stick
- 3 Cardamom pods, lightly smashed
- 6 Bone-in, skin-on chicken thighs
- 3 Tbsp. fish sauce
- 1 Tbsp. sugar
- 8 ½ Cups of water
- Kosher salt
- Freshly ground black pepper
- 4 Servings rice noodles, prepared according to package directions

Toppings:

- 3 Scallions, sliced
- 1 Small handful fresh herbs, such as mint, cilantro, and Thai basil, chopped
- 1 Lime, cut into wedges
- Handful of bean sprouts (optional)
- 1 Jalapeño, thinly sliced (optional)

Cooking Instructions:

1. Preheat the Instant Pot by selecting Sauté on high heat. Once hot, add the oil to the pot.

2. Add the onions, cut-side down, and the ginger. Cook without moving for about 4 minutes or until charred.

3. Add the coriander, star anise, cloves, cinnamon stick, and cardamom. Stir and cook for additional 1 minute.

4. Add the chicken, fish sauce, and sugar and immediately pour over the water. Secure the lid.

5. Select the Manual high pressure button to cook for 18 minutes. When timer beeps, use natural pressure release for about 10 minutes, then release any remaining pressure.

6. Remove the chicken from the pot and carefully strain the broth. Season with salt and pepper if desired. Flip the noodles onto serving plates.

7. When the chicken is cool enough to handle, pick the meat off the bones and add to the bowls.

8. Pour over the broth and top with scallions, herbs, lime, and bean sprouts and jalapeño (if using).

9. Serve and enjoy!

Italian Beef Stew

Preparation time: 10 minutes

Cook time: 35 minutes

Total time: 45 minutes

Serves: 5

Ingredients:

- 3 Lbs. beef stew meat OR 2 lbs. of ground beef, browned.
- 1 Onion
- 4 Carrots
- 8 Oz. fresh baby portabella mushrooms (optional)
- 24 Oz. beef broth
- 15 Oz. can diced tomatoes
- 3 Tbsp. flour
- 1 Tsp. dried basil leaves
- 1 Tsp. dried thyme leaves
- 1 Tsp. salt
- 1 Tsp. pepper Dried parsley

Cooking Instructions:

1. Dice 1 onion, 4 carrots and slice 8 oz. mushrooms.

2. Add meat in Instant Pot. If you are using ground beef, sauté then drain grease.

3. Add carrots, broth, flour, basil, thyme, salt, pepper and diced tomatoes to Instant Pot; stir.

4. Place lid on Instant pot and close valve. Select the Manual high pressure button to cook for 35 minutes.

5. When timer beeps, use natural pressure release for about 10 minutes, then release any remaining pressure.

6. Remove the lid and stir in mushrooms (if you have them).

7. Serve and enjoy!

Vegetable Soup

Preparation time: 8 minutes

Cook time: 15 minutes

Total time: 23 minutes

Serves: 8

Ingredients:

- 2 Stalks celery
- 6 Carrots
- ½ Large onion
- 12 Oz. frozen okra
- 12 Oz. frozen green beans
- 12 Oz. frozen corn
- 12 Oz. frozen peas
- 4 Cups of beef broth

Cooking Instructions:

1. Wash and chop up the celery, onions and carrots.
2. Add all the chopped and frozen veggies to the Instant Pot.
3. Add beef broth to the Instant Pot. You can either use broth you have saved from a roast, or you can use a beef base or bullion to make a broth.
4. Secure the lid on the Instant Pot and secure in place.
5. Select the Soup button to cook for 35 minutes.
6. Serve and enjoy!

Italian Sausage Stew

Preparation time: 10 minutes

Cook time: 10 minutes

Total time: 20 minutes

Serves: 5

Ingredients:

- 2 Tbsp. butter
- ½ Lb. pastured ground pork
- ½ Tsp. onion powder
- ½ Tsp. garlic powder
- 1½ Tsp. basil
- ½ Tsp. thyme
- ¼ Tsp. cumin
- ½ Tsp. marjoram
- ¼ Tsp. cayenne
- 1 Tsp. sea salt
- ¼ Tsp. black pepper
- 1 Medium onion, diced
- 2 Carrots, diced
- 2 Stalks of celery, diced
- 4 Cloves of garlic, minced
- ½ Cup of white wine
- 13 Oz. can organic diced tomatoes
- 2 Quarts bone broth
- 3 Large handfuls kale, chopped
- 8 Oz. gluten free noodles
- Sea salt/pepper to taste
- Freshly grated parm or other raw cheese to garnish

Cooking Instructions:

1. Set the Instant Pot to "sauté".

2. Once the bottom is warm put butter to melt and then add the pork and all of the seasonings.

3. Stir to combine and brown the meat. Add the onion, carrot, celery, and garlic, combine and cook for 6-8 minutes until the veggies are soft and sweet.

4. Add the white wine to deglaze the pan scraping up any bits at the bottom.

5. Add the diced tomatoes, broth, kale and noodles and stir to combine. Secure the lid on Instant Pot making sure the valve is sealed.

6. Select the Manual high pressure key to cook for 3 minutes. When timer beeps, use natural pressure release for about 10 minutes, then release any remaining pressure.

7. Season with salt and pepper to taste. Flip onto serving plates with freshly grated parmesan.

8. Serve and enjoy!

Cheddar Broccoli and Potato Soup

Preparation time: 10 minutes

Cook time: 15 minutes

Total time: 25 minutes

Serves: 5

Ingredients:

- 2 Tbsp. butter
- 2 Cloves garlic, crushed
- 1 Medium sized broccoli head, broken into large florets
- 2 Lbs. Yukon Gold Potatoes, peeled and cut into small chunks
- 4 Cups of vegetable or chicken broth, plus more if needed
- Salt and Pepper to taste
- 1 Cup of half and half
- 1 Cup of shredded cheddar cheese
- 6 Slices of bacon (optional)
- Chopped green onion or chives for garnish

Cooking Instructions:

1. Select the sauté function on the Instant Pot.

2. Once hot, add butter and crushed garlic. Sauté about one minute, or until garlic begins to brown.

3. Add broccoli, potatoes, and broth. Season with extra salt and pepper. Secure the lid and select Manual High Pressure to cook for about 5 minutes.

4. Once cooking is complete, select cancel and use the natural pressure release for 10 minutes. Remove any remaining steam.

5. If using bacon, microwave or cook the bacon until desired crispiness. Set aside to cool. Add the half and half and ½ cup of cheddar cheese.

6. Blend with an immersion blender until smooth, or blend in batches in a large blender. If you want a thinner soup, add more broth.

7. Add salt and pepper to taste. Flip onto serving plates with remaining cheddar and bacon (if using).

8. Serve and enjoy!

Spanish Infused Chicken Stew

Preparation time: 10 minutes

Cook time: 10 minutes

Total time: 20 minutes

Serves: 4

Ingredients:

- 4 Large chicken breasts, cut into chunks
- 4 Cloves of garlic, minced
- ½ Cooking chorizo, chopped roughly
- 2 Carrots, chopped roughly
- 2 Courgettes, chopped roughly
- 2 Leeks, chopped roughly
- 3 Red skinned potatoes, scrubbed and chopped in half
- 1 Can of cannellini beans
- 1 Handful of parsley, roughly chopped
- A small handful of oregano, finely chopped
- Glass of fino sherry or dry white wine, and one for yourself
- A large pinch of smoked paprika
- A couple of strands of saffron
- Salt and pepper to taste
- Chicken stock, enough to cover the chicken and vegetables

Cooking Instructions:

1. Prepare the vegetables and place them in the Instant Pot.

2. Heat some oil in a sauté pan and sauté the garlic, chicken and chorizo until the chicken is browned.

3. Add the chicken, chorizo and garlic mixture to the Instant Pot and stir. Heat the stock slightly and add the herbs, spices, seasonings and pour over the chicken to cover it.

4. Secure the lid and select the Manual high pressure key to cook for 10 minutes. When timer beeps, use natural pressure release for about 10 minutes.

5. Quick release any remaining pressure. Check for seasoning and flip onto serving plates with crusty bread or rice.

6. Serve and enjoy!

Chicken Noodle Soup

Preparation time: 10 minutes

Cook time: 15 minutes

Total time: 25 minutes

Serves: 5

Ingredients:

- 3 Tbsp. salted butter
- 1 ¼ Cups of onion, chopped
- 4 Cloves garlic, chopped
- 1 ¼ Cups of carrots, chopped
- 1 ¼ Cups of celery chopped
- 1 lb. Chicken cooked and chopped
- 4 Cups of chicken broth
- 1 Package home-style noodles
- Dash of celery salt, optional

Cooking Instructions:

1. Cook chicken beforehand in Instant Pot, remove and set aside.

2. Wash and chop carrots, celery, onion, and garlic.

3. Sauté all the vegetables in butter in the Instant Pot for about 3 minutes or until soft.

4. Add chopped chicken and broth, stirring well.

5. Add noodles and cook until the noodles are done.

6. Add a dash of celery salt, if desired.

7. Serve and enjoy!

Tomato Chick Pea Soup

Preparation time: 12 minutes

Cook time: 8 minutes

Total time: 20 minutes

Serves: 4

Ingredients:

- 3 Tbsp. Olive Oil
- 2 Onions
- 3 Celery Stalks
- 3 Carrots
- 1 Red Bell Pepper
- 1 Tbsp. Turmeric
- 1 Tbsp. ground Coriander
- 1 Tsp. ground Cinnamon
- 1 Garlic Clove (minced)
- 30 Oz. of canned or fresh tomatoes
- 1 Zucchini
- 2 Cups of broth (vegetable or bone)
- 2 Cans Chickpeas (garbanzo beans)
- Salt and pepper
- Garnish with Lime wedges, green onions or cilantro (optional)

Cooking Instructions:

1. Clean and dice the onions, celery, carrots, and red peppers.

2. Press the sauté button on the Instant Pot. Once Instant Pot is hot, add butter, oil, onions and carrots.

3. Sauté for about 6 minutes or until the onions become translucent. Add the celery and red bell pepper along with the dry spices.

4. Stir in the garlic, tomatoes, and zucchini. Rinse the chickpeas and add to mixture. Add enough broth to cover vegetables.

5. Season with Salt and Pepper to taste. Secure the lid into place and set venting button to sealed position. Select the Manual high pressure key to cook for 10 minutes.

6. When timer beeps, use natural pressure release for about 5 minutes, then release any remaining pressure.

7. Stir well and add additional broth if needed. Just before serving squeeze the lime over the top or offer lime wedges with soup plates.

8. Serve and enjoy!

Irish Stew

Preparation time: 7 minutes

Cook time: 8 minutes

Total time: 13 minutes

Serves: 5

Ingredients:

- ½ Cup of beef broth
- ½ Cup of Guinness or other dark stout
- 2 Lbs. boneless lamb or stew beef, trim off extra fat and cube into about 1 inch pieces
- 12 Small red potatoes, wash well and cut in half or quarters if larger
- 14 Oz. can diced tomatoes
- 1 Chopped onion
- 4 Carrots, sliced into half inch rounds
- 3 Parsnips, sliced into half inch rounds
- 2 Small turnips, sliced in half and into half inch strips
- 2 Bay leaves
- 1 Tsp. salt
- 1 Tsp. black pepper
- 1 Tsp. minced garlic (fresh or jarred)
- 4 Tbsp. all-purpose flour
- 16 Oz. bag frozen peas
- ¼ Cup of chopped fresh parsley

Cooking Instructions:

1. Sprinkle lamb cubes (or stew beef) with salt, pepper, and garlic.

2. Mix well to cover all pieces and set aside. Wash and slice potatoes, carrots, onion, parsnips, and turnips.

3. Place broth, stout or extra broth into the Instant Pot liner. Add the lamb (or stew beef), potatoes, carrots, onion, parsnips, turnips, and tomatoes to liner.

4. Gently mix with large spoon. Add bay leaves. Lock lid in place and make sure vent button is turned to the closed position.

5. Select the Manual high pressure key to cook for 20 minutes. When timer beeps, use natural pressure release for about 10 minutes, then release any remaining pressure.

6. While the stew is coming up to a boil, place flour and 1.2 cup of water into a covered dish or jar and shake to combine.

7. Pour into stew and gently stir until the stew thickens.

8. Serve and enjoy!

Creamy Thai Coconut Chicken Soup

Preparation time: 6 minutes

Cook time: 8 minutes

Total time: 14 minutes

Serves: 6

Ingredients:

- 2 Tbsp. oil
- 1 Small onion, quartered
- 2 Lbs. skinless and boneless chicken breast or chicken thighs, cut into cubes
- 2 Tbsp. Thai red curry paste (Mae Ploy brand)
- 1 Red bell pepper, cut into thick strips
- Slices galangal, optional
- 6 Kaffir lime leaves, torn and bruised, optional
- 3 Cups chicken broth
- 2 Tbsp. fish sauce or salt to taste
- 1 Heaping tablespoon sugar
- ¾ Cup of coconut milk
- 2 ½ Tbsp. lime juice
- Cilantro leaves

Cooking Instructions:

1. Turn on the Sauté mode on your Instant Pot.

2. Add the onion and sauté for 10 seconds before adding the chicken. Sauté the chicken until the surface turns white.

3. Add the Thai curry paste, bell peppers, galangal and kaffir lime leaves (if using), stir to mix well.

4. Add the chicken broth, fish sauce and sugar. Secure the lid and select Manual High pressure button to cook for 6 minutes.

5. When timer beeps, use natural pressure release for about 10 minutes, then release any remaining pressure.

6. Remove the lid carefully, add the coconut milk and lime juice to the soup, stir to mix well. Top with cilantro.

7. Serve and enjoy!

Smoky Lentil and Potato Soup

Preparation time: 14 minutes

Cook time: 5 minutes

Total time: 19 minutes

Serves: 4

Ingredients:

- 1 Tbsp. olive oil
- ½ Cup chopped yellow or white onion
- 3 Cloves garlic, finely minced or pressed through a garlic press
- ½ Cup of diced carrots (about 2 medium carrots)
- 1/2 Cup of diced celery (about 2 stalks)
- 2 Tsp. ground cumin
- 1 ½ Tsp. smoked paprika
- 1 Tsp. salt
- 1 Lb. Yukon Gold or red potatoes, cut into 1-inch pieces
- 1 Cup of red lentils, sorted and rinsed
- 1 Cup of brown lentils, sorted and rinsed
- 2 Cups chicken or vegetable stock or broth
- 10 Oz kale or spinach, chopped (optional)

Cooking Instructions:

1. Heat the oil using the Sauté function in the Instant Pot.

2. Add the onion, garlic, carrots, and celery, and cook for a minute or two, stirring constantly so the garlic does not burn.

3. Add the cumin, paprika and salt. Stir to combine. Add the potatoes, lentils and stock or broth.

4. Secure the lid and select Manual High pressure button to cook for 5 minutes.

5. When timer beeps, use natural pressure release for about 10 minutes, then release any remaining pressure.

6. Open the lid, and stir in the kale or spinach, if using. Season to taste with salt and pepper.

7. Serve and enjoy!

INSTANT POT FISH & SEAFOOD RECIPES

Shrimp Scampi

Preparation time: 10 minutes

Cook time: 5 minutes

Total time: 15 minutes

Serves: 4

Ingredients:

- 1 ½ Lb. jumbo shrimp, peeled, deveined
- ¼ Cup of dry white wine
- Garlic cloves, finely chopped
- 2 Tsp. kosher salt
- 1/4 Tsp. freshly ground black pepper
- Tbsp. unsalted butter
- ¼ Cup of finely chopped parsley
- 2 Tsp. fresh lemon juice

Cooking Instructions:

1. Add the shrimp, wine, and garlic into Instant Pot; season with salt and pepper.

2. Secure the lid making sure steam-release valve is in the proper sealed position. Select "Manual High Pressure" to cook for 5 minutes.

3. When timer beeps, use natural pressure release for about 8 minutes, then release any remaining pressure.

4. Using a slotted spoon, transfer shrimp to a medium bowl, leaving juices behind.

5. Select "Sauté" and simmer liquid until reduced by half, about 6 minutes. Add butter and stir until melted and incorporated and sauce is thick.

6. Return shrimp to pot, add parsley and lemon juice, and toss to combine. Flip onto serving plates.

7. Serve and enjoy!

Steamed Alaskan Crab Legs

Preparation time: 8 minutes

Cook time: 5 minutes

Total time: 13 minutes

Serves: 5

Ingredients:

- 3 Lbs. frozen crab legs
- 1 Cup of water
- ½ Tbsp. salt
- Melted butter for serving

Cooking Instructions:

1. Place steamer basket into Instant Pot with 1 cup of water and ½ tbsp. of salt.

2. Add half of the Alaskan King Crab Legs with 1 tbsp. of salt.

3. Secure the lid of the Instant Pot and ensure the valve is set to sealing position.

4. Press Manual High Pressure to cook for 4 minutes.

5. When timer beeps, use natural pressure release for about 5 minutes, then release any remaining pressure.

6. Remove crab legs and put in serving plates with melted butter. Repeat process with remaining half of crab legs.

7. Serve and enjoy!

10-Minute Instant Pot Salmon

Preparation time: 10 minutes

Cook time: 5 minutes

Total time: 15 minutes

Serves: 4

Ingredients:

- 1 Medium – lemon
- ¾ Cup of water
- Fillet – salmon
- 1 Bunch off dill weed, fresh
- 1 Tbsp. butter, unsalted
- ¼ Tsp. salt
- ¼ Tsp. black pepper, ground

Optional:

- 1 Cup of brown rice, raw
- 1 Cup of green beans

Cooking Instructions:

1. Place ¼ cup of fresh lemon juice, plus ¾ cup of water in the bottom of the Instant Pot.

2. Add the metal steamer insert. Place the (Sockeye) salmon fillets, frozen, on top of the steamer insert.

3. Sprinkle fresh dill on top of the salmon, then place one slice of fresh lemon on top of each.

4. Lock the Instant Pot lid. Press Manual High Pressure to cook for 5 minutes. When timer beeps, use natural pressure release for about 5 minutes, then release any remaining pressure.

5. Flip onto serving plates, top with butter, extra dill lemon, salt or pepper.

6. Serve and enjoy!

Shrimp Paella

Preparation time: 10 minutes

Cook time: 5 minutes

Total time: 15 minutes

Serves: 4

Calories 318 kcal

Ingredients:

- 1 Lb. jumbo shrimp, shell and tail on frozen
- 1 Cup of Jasmine rice
- 1 Tbsp. butter
- 1 Onion, chopped
- Cloves garlic, chopped
- 1 Red pepper, chopped
- 1 Cup of chicken broth
- ½ Cup of white wine
- 1 Tsp. paprika
- 1 Tsp. turmeric
- ½ Tsp. salt
- ¼ Tsp. black pepper
- 1 Pinch saffron threads
- ¼ Tsp red pepper flakes
- ¼ Cup of cilantro optional

Cooking Instructions:

1. Set Instant Pot to Sauté function. Add butter to pot and melt.

2. Add onions and cook until softened. Add garlic and cook for about a minute more.

3. Add paprika, turmeric, salt, black pepper, red pepper flakes, and saffron threads. Stir and cook for about 1 minute.

4. Add red peppers. Add rice and stir. Cook for about 30 seconds to 1 minute. Add chicken broth and white wine, making sure all rice is covered.

5. Add shrimp on top. Secure the lid and Make sure valve is set to sealing position. Set Instant Pot to Manual High Pressure mode to cook for about 5 minutes.

6. When timer beeps, use natural pressure release for about 5 minutes, then release any remaining pressure.

7   Remove shrimp from pot and peel if desired and top with Cilantro.

8   Serve and enjoy!

Coconut Fish Curry

Preparation time: 6 minutes

Cook time: 15 minutes

Total time: 21 minutes

Serves: 4

Ingredients:

- 1-1.5 Lb. (500-750g) Fish steaks or fillets, rinsed and cut into bite-size pieces (fresh or frozen and thawed)
- 1 Tomato, chopped (or a heaping cup of cherry tomatoes)
- 2 Green Chiles, sliced into strips
- 2 Medium onions, sliced into strips
- 2 Garlic cloves, squeezed
- 1 Tbsp. freshly grated Ginger, (or ⅛ tsp. ginger powder)
- Curry leaves, or Bay Laurel Leaves, or Kaffir Lime Leaves, or Basil
- 1 Tbsp. ground Coriander
- 2 Tsp. ground Cumin
- ½ Tsp. ground Turmeric
- 1 Tsp. Chili powder, or 1 tsp. of Hot Pepper Flakes
- ½ Tsp. Ground Fenugreek (Methi)

Optional Toppings:

- 2 Cups (500ml) of unsweetened Coconut Milk
- 2 Tsp Salt to taste
- Lemon juice to taste (I used the juice from ½ lemon)

Cooking Instructions:

1. Heat the Instant Pot with oil, put the curry leaves and lightly fry them until golden around the edges (about 1 minute).

2. Add the onion, garlic, and ginger and sauté until the onion is soft. Add all of the ground spices: Coriander, Cumin, Turmeric, Chili Powder, and Fenugreek.

3. Sauté them together with the onions until they have released their aroma (about 2 minutes).

4. Deglaze with the coconut milk making sure to un-stick anything from the bottom of the Instant Pot and incorporate it into the sauce.

5   Add the Green chilies, tomatoes and fish pieces. Stir to coat the fish well with the mixture. Close the lid and set the valve to sealing position.

6   Cook for 5 minutes at Low Pressure. When timer beeps, use natural pressure release for about 5 minutes, then release any remaining pressure.

7   Add salt to taste and top with lemon juice.

8   Serve and enjoy!

Chipotle Shrimp Soup

Preparation time: 6 minutes

Cook time: 25 minutes

Total time: 31 minutes

Serves: 5

Ingredients:

- Slices of bacon, chopped
- 1 Cup of onion, diced
- ¾ Cup of celery, chopped
- 1 Tsp. garlic
- 1 Tbsp. flour
- ¼ Cup of dry white wine
- 1 ½ Cups of chicken or vegetable broth
- ½ Cup of whole milk
- 1 ½ Cups of potatoes, cut into small (1/3-inch) cubes
- 1 Cup of frozen corn kernels
- 2 Tsp. diced canned chipotle peppers in adobo sauce
- ¾ Tsp. salt (or to taste)
- ½ Tsp. ground black pepper
- ½ Tsp. dried thyme
- ½ Lb. shrimp, peeled and deveined
- ¼ Cup of heavy cream

Cooking Instructions:

1. Select the 'Sauté' function. Add bacon into Instant Pot and sauté until crisp (about 3 minutes), stirring frequently.

2. Add onions, celery and garlic. Sauté until vegetables have softened, (about 3 minutes).

3. Stir in flour and cook for about a minute. Press 'Cancel' and add white wine to deglaze the pot.

4. Stir to remove brown bits from the bottom of the Instant Pot. Stir in broth, milk, potatoes, corn, chipotle, salt, black pepper and thyme.

5. Close the lid and select 'Manual High Pressure' to cook for 1 minute. When timer beeps, use natural pressure release for about 5 minutes, then release any remaining pressure.

6   Stir in shrimp and cream. Secure the lid in place and allow the shrimp to cook in the residual heat for 10 minutes.

7   Flip onto serving plates and garnish with scallions, parsley and/or crumbled bacon.

8   Serve and enjoy!

Cajun Shrimp and Sausage Boil

Preparation time: 10 minutes

Cook time: 10 minutes

Total time: 20 minutes

Serves: 5

Calories: 459 kcal

Ingredients:

- ½ Lb. smoked sausage, cut into four pieces
- Ears corn
- 2 Red potatoes, cut in half
- 1 Tbsp. Louisiana Shrimp and Crab Boil
- Water to cover the above
- ½ Lb. raw shrimp

For Sauce:

- 1 Tbsp. butter
- 1 Tbsp. garlic, minced
- 1/8 Tsp. Cajun seasoning
- ¼ Tsp. Old Bay seasoning
- 5 Shakes hot sauce, such as Louisiana Hot sauce or Tabasco
- 1/8 Tsp. lemon pepper
- ½ Lemon, juiced

Cooking Instructions:

1. Place the sausage, corn, and potatoes in the pot and cover with water.

2. Add in the Louisiana Shrimp and Crab Boil Mix. Set Instant Pot to Manual High pressure to cook for 4 minutes.

3. Meanwhile, in a pan over medium-high heat, melt the butter. Add minced garlic and sauté well while stirring, allowing the butter to boil and take on the garlic flavor.

4. Add all other spices, mix well and taste it. Leave this sauce to warm in the pan. By this time your Instant Pot should be done.

5. When timer beeps, use natural pressure release for about 10 minutes, then release any remaining pressure.

6   Check to ensure the potatoes are cooked. Add your shrimp and stir. As soon as the shrimp turns pink, take them out and then take out the corn, potatoes, and sausage.

7   Put everything into the sauce one after the other, stirring well to coat everything with the spiced butter goodness, starting with the shrimp so they have to cook just a little more.

8   Serve and enjoy!

Lemon Pepper Salmon

Preparation time: 5 minutes

Cook time: 10 minutes

Total time: 15 minutes

Serves: 5

Ingredients:

- ¾ Cup of water
- A few sprigs of parsley dill, tarragon, basil or a combo
- 1 Lb. salmon filet skin on
- 1 TSP. ghee or other healthy fat divided
- ¼ Tsp. salt or to taste
- ½ Tsp. pepper or to taste
- 1/2 Lemon thinly sliced
- 1 Zucchini julienned
- 1 Red bell pepper julienned
- 1 Carrot julienned

Cooking Instructions:

1. Put water and herbs in the Instant Pot and then put in the steamer rack making sure the handles are extended up.

2. Place salmon, skin down on rack. Drizzle salmon with ghee/fat, season with salt and pepper and cover with lemon slices

3. Secure the lid on Instant Pot and make sure vent is turned to "Sealing position". Select "Manual High Pressure" to cook for 5 minutes.

4. While salmon cooks, julienne your veggies. When timer beeps, use natural pressure release for about 10 minutes, then release any remaining pressure.

5. Remove lid, and using hot pads, carefully remove rack with salmon and set on a plate. Remove herbs and discard.

6. Add veggies and put the lid back on. Press "Sauté" and let the veggies cook for just 1 or 2 minutes. Flip onto serving bowl.

7. Serve and enjoy!

Crustless Crab Quiche

Preparation time: 15 minutes

Cook time: 50 minutes

Total time: 1 hour 5 minutes

Serves: 5

Calories: 395 kcal

Ingredients:

- 4 Eggs
- 1 Cup of half and half
- 1 Tsp. salt
- 1 Tsp. pepper
- 1 Tsp. sweet smoked paprika
- 1 Tsp. Simply Organic Herbes de Provence, 1 Oz. Herbes de Provence
- 1 Cup of shredded parmesan or Swiss cheese
- 1 Cup of chopped green onions green and white parts
- 8 Oz. imitation crab meat about 2 cups OR
- 8 Oz. real crab meat, or a mix of crab and chopped raw shrimp

Cooking Instructions:

1. In a large bowl, beat together eggs and half-and-half with a whisk.

2. Add salt, pepper, sweet smoked paprika, Herbes de Provence, and shredded cheese, and stir with a fork to mix. Stir in chopped green onions.

3. Add either the imitation crab meat or the real crab meat or some combination of crab meat and chopped raw shrimp.

4. Lay out a sheet of aluminum foil that is cut bigger than the pan you intend to use. Place the spring form pan on this sheet and crimp the sheet about the bottom.

5. You are doing this as most spring form pans can leak a little with liquids. The aluminum foil reduces the mess a little.

6. Pour the egg mixture into your spring form pan. Cover loosely with foil or a silicone lid. Into the inner pot of Instant Pot, place 2 cups of water.

7. Place a steamer rack in the pot. Place the covered spring form pan on the trivet. Select "Manual High Pressure" button to cook for 5 minutes.

8 When timer beeps, use natural pressure release for about 10 minutes, then release any remaining pressure.

9 Take out the hot silicone pan. Using a knife, loosen the edges of the quiche from the pan. Remove the outer ring.

10 Serve and enjoy!

Lobster Bisque

Preparation time: 5 minutes

Cook time: 9 minutes

Total time: 14 minutes

Serves: 4

Ingredients:

- 2 Carrots, diced
- 1 Diced celery
- 29 Oz. canned petite diced tomatoes
- 2 Whole Shallots, Minced
- 1 Clove Garlic, Minced
- 1 Tbsp. Butter
- 32 Oz. low-sodium chicken broth
- 1 Tbsp. Old Bay Seasoning
- 1 Tsp. Dried Dill
- 1 Tsp. Freshly Ground Black Pepper
- ½ Tsp Paprika
- Lobster Tails (or 24 oz. frozen lobster)
- 1 Pint Heavy Whipping Cream

Cooking Instructions:

1. Place butter, minced shallots and garlic into Instant Pot and sauté for 2-3 minutes, or until shallots and garlic are translucent.

2. Add the tomatoes, carrots, celery, minced shallots and garlic into the Instant Pot. Add chicken broth and spices to the Instant Pot.

3. If you're using full lobster tails, use a knife to cut off the fan at the end of the lobster and add those to the pot, otherwise place the frozen lobster into the Instant Pot.

4. Select "Manual High Pressure" button to cook for 5 minutes. When timer beeps, use natural pressure release for about 8 minutes, then release any remaining pressure.

5. If you've used lobster tails take them from the pot and remove the flesh from the tails at this time.

6. Using an immersion blender, puree the soup mixture to desired chunkiness. Add the cream and stir. Serve and enjoy!

INSTANT POT POULTRY RECIPES

Teriyaki Chicken & Rice

Preparation time: 5 minutes

Cook time: 25 minutes

Total time: 30 minutes

Serves: 4

Ingredients:

- 2 Cups of low sodium chicken broth
- 1/3 Cup of low sodium soy sauce
- ¼ Cup of hoisin sauce
- 1 Tbsp. white vinegar
- 1 Tbsp. liquid honey
- 2 Tsp minced garlic
- 1 Tsp minced ginger
- 1 Pinch red pepper flakes optional
- 1 ½ Cups of long grain brown rice
- 2 Boneless skinless chicken breasts
- 1 Red bell pepper chopped
- 1 Large carrot finely diced
- 1 Cup of frozen peas

Cooking Instructions:

1. Add the broth, soy sauce, hoisin sauce, vinegar, honey, garlic, ginger and pepper into Instant Pot and stir well.

2. Add the rice and place the chicken breasts on top. Secure the lid and make sure the valve is set to sealing position.

3. Select Manual High Pressure to cook for 20 minutes. When timer beeps, use natural pressure release for about 10 minutes, then release any remaining pressure.

4. Serve and enjoy!

Salsa Lime Chicken

Preparation time: 5 minutes

Cook time: 25 minutes

Total time: 30 minutes

Serves: 6

Ingredients:

- Chicken breasts
- 16 Oz. Salsa
- Juice from 1 large lime

Cooking Instructions:

1. Add the chicken breasts in the Instant Pot.

2. Pour salsa over the chicken. Pour lime juice over the top of the salsa.

3. Cover the lid, Click on the Poultry Setting and set timer for 25 minutes.

5. When timer beeps, use natural pressure release for about 10 minutes, then release any remaining pressure.

6. Serve and enjoy!

Chicken Adobo

Preparation time: 5 minutes

Cook time: 35 minutes

Total time: 40 minutes

Serves: 5

Ingredients:

- Chicken drumsticks
- Salt and pepper
- 2 Tbsp. avocado oil (or other higher heat oil such as canola)
- ½ Yellow onion sliced
- 12 Garlic gloves peeled and chopped
- ½ Cup of soy sauce
- ½ Cup of distilled white vinegar (apple cider vinegar is also a good alternative)
- ¼ Cup of water
- Bay leaves
- 1 ½ Tsp. coarse ground black pepper

Cooking Instructions:

1. Season chicken drumsticks with salt and pepper.

2. With the sauté feature on, heat oil and cook chicken pieces, in batches if necessary until browned on all sides.

3. If you cooked the chicken in batches, return all chicken to the pot. Add in remaining ingredients.

4. Secure the lid and make sure the valve is set to sealing position. Select Manual High Pressure to cook for 30 minutes.

5. When timer beeps, use natural pressure release for about 10 minutes, then release any remaining pressure.

6. Remove bay leaves. Flip chicken to serving plates with rice and sauce.

7. Serve and enjoy!

Buffalo Chicken Soup with Crumbled Blue Cheese

Preparation time: 10 minutes

Cook time: 15 minutes

Total time: 25 minutes

Serves: 6

Ingredients:

- 1 Large onion chopped small
- 2 Cups of chopped celery, chopped small
- 1 T olive oil
- 1 Tsp. dried thyme (grinded)
- 1 Tsp. garlic powder
- Boneless, skinless chicken breasts, trimmed and cut into lengthwise strips
- 1 Cup of Frank's Red Hot Sauce
- 2 Cups of chicken stock
- 5 Oz. cream cheese, cut into small cubes
- ½ Cup of crumbled blue cheese, plus more for serving

Cooking Instructions:

1. Chop the onion and celery. Heat the oil in the Instant Pot, using the Sauté setting with medium heat.

2. Add the chopped onion and celery and cook until they are soften, about 5 minutes. Add the thyme, garlic powder and cook a minute or two longer.

3. While the veggies cook, trim the chicken and cut into lengthwise strips. Add the chicken strips, Frank's Red Hot Sauce, and chicken stock to the Instant Pot.

4. Secure the lid and make sure the valve is set to sealing position. Select Manual High Pressure to cook for 15 minutes.

5. When timer beeps, use natural pressure release for about 10 minutes, then release any remaining pressure.

6. Use a slotted spoon to remove the chicken to a cutting board and shred apart. While the soup cooks, crumble the blue cheese and cut the cream cheese into small cubes.

7. After the pressure has released and you've removed the chicken to a cutting board, add the two cheeses to the Instant Pot.

8. Allow them to melt while you shred the chicken apart. When cheeses have melted, whisk soup together, then add the shredded chicken back into the soup.

9. Share the soup into serving plates with extra crumbled blue cheese and Frank's Red Hot Sauce to add at the table if desired.

10. Serve and enjoy!

Honey Garlic Chicken

Preparation time: 5 minutes

Cook time: 27 minutes

Total time: 32 minutes

Serves: 4

Calories: 360 kcal

Ingredients:

- ⅓ Cup of honey
- Cloves garlic, minced
- ½ Cup of low sodium soy sauce
- ½ Cup of no salt ketchup
- ½ Tsp. dried oregano
- 2 Tbsp. chopped fresh parsley
- 1 Tbsp. sesame seed oil
- Bone-in, skinless chicken thighs
- Salt and fresh ground pepper, to taste
- ½ Tbsp. toasted sesame seeds, for garnish
- Sliced green onions, for garnish

Cooking Instructions:

1. In a small mixing bowl combine honey, minced garlic, soy sauce, ketchup, oregano and parsley; mix until well combined and set aside.

2. Heat the Instant Pot in sauté mode. Add sesame oil to the pot. Season chicken thighs with salt and pepper.

3. Carefully arrange in the Instant Pot and cook for about 2 to 3 minutes per side. Add the prepared honey garlic sauce to the pot; cover and lock the lid.

4. Press Poultry mode to cook for 20 minutes. When timer beeps, use natural pressure release for about 5 minutes, then release any remaining pressure.

5. Flip chicken to a serving plate and spoon the sauce over the chicken. Garnish with toasted sesame seeds and green onions.

6. Serve and enjoy!

Mongolian Chicken

Preparation time: 12 minutes

Cook time: 25 minutes

Total time: 37 minutes

Serves: 4

Ingredients:

- Boneless skinless chicken breasts cut into one-two inch cubes
- 2 Tbsp. extra virgin olive oil
- ¾ Cup of brown sugar (use less if you want)
- Garlic cloves, minced
- 1 Tbsp. fresh ginger minced
- ¾ Cup of lite soy sauce (use ½ cup if you are sensitive to sodium)
- ¾ Cup of water or chicken broth
- 1 Cup of carrots chopped
- 1 Tsp. red pepper flakes
- 1 Tbsp. garlic powder
- 2 Tbsp. cornstarch

Optional:

- ¼ Cup green onions chopped
- 1 Tsp. sesame seeds
- Rice (optional):
- 2 Cups of basmati rice
- 2 Cups of water
- 2 Tbsp. herbed or unsalted butter
- ¼ Tsp. salt

Cooking Instructions:

1. Heat the Instant Pot using Sauté function. Add the oil to the Instant Pot.

2. Add the chicken and sauté for about 3 minutes, stirring for sometimes. Cook until it just starts to get golden.

3. When sautéing it, stir constantly so it doesn't stick to the bottom of the pan. Deglaze the pot with ¼ cup water and scrape them with a wooden spoon.

4. Add the rest of the ingredients to the pot: minced garlic, ginger, lite soy sauce, brown sugar, water, carrots, garlic powder and red pepper flakes.

5   Stir well until all the ingredients are combined and coated in sauce. Secure the lid and make sure the valve is set to sealing position.

6   Select Manual High Pressure to cook for 3 minutes. When timer beeps, use natural pressure release for about 10 minutes, then release any remaining pressure.

7   Serve and enjoy!

Creamy Italian Chicken Breasts

Preparation time: 10 minutes

Cook time: 10 minutes

Total time: 20 minutes

Serves: 4

Calories: 238 k

Ingredients:

- Boneless skinless chicken breasts
- 1 Cup of low sodium chicken broth
- 1 Tsp. minced garlic
- 1 Tsp. Italian seasoning
- ¼ Tsp. salt
- ¼ Tsp. black pepper
- 1/3 Cup of heavy cream
- 1/3 Cup of roasted red peppers
- 1 ½ Tbsp. corn starch
- 1 Tbsp. basil pesto

Cooking Instructions:

1. Place chicken breasts in the bottom of the Instant Pot.

2. Add broth and sprinkle with garlic, Italian seasoning, salt and pepper. Secure the lid and make sure the valve is set to sealing position.

3. Select Manual High Pressure to cook for 10 minutes. When timer beeps, use natural pressure release for about 5 minutes, then release any remaining pressure.

4. Remove the chicken breasts and place on a cutting board or serving platter. Turn the Instant Pot to sauté.

5. Stir together cream, red peppers, corn starch and pesto and add to the pot. Whisk and cook for 4 minutes, until thickened. Add chicken back to the sauce.

6. Serve and enjoy!

Chicken Marsala

Preparation time: 5 minutes

Cook time: 10 minutes

Total time: 15 minutes

Serves: 4

Ingredients:

- 1 Tbsp. butter
- Flour for dredging
- 1 Lb. thinly sliced chicken breasts
- Oz. sliced mushrooms
- Oz. pancetta, finely cubed
- 2/3 Cup of marsala cooking wine
- 1 Cup of chicken broth
- 2 Cloves garlic, minced
- 1 Tbsp. cornstarch + 1 Tbsp. water
- Fresh parsley to garnish

Cooking Instructions:

1. Turn Instant Pot to sauté function and add butter to melt.

2. Dredge chicken breasts in flour on both sides, then place into Instant Pot. Let them brown in the butter for 1-2 minutes per side, then remove and set aside.

3. Add garlic, pancetta, mushrooms and masala wine and sauté for 2 minutes. Turn Instant Pot off. Add chicken breasts back in, along with chicken broth, nestling chicken down into the mushrooms.

4. Secure the lid and make sure the valve is set to sealing position. Select Manual High Pressure button to cook for 8 minutes.

5. When timer beeps, use natural pressure release for about 5 minutes, then release any remaining pressure. Remove just the chicken breasts from the pot and switch the Instant Pot to sauté.

6. Wait for 1 minute until sauce starts to bubble. Add the mixture of cornstarch and water and let simmer 5-10 minutes, stirring occasionally while sauce thickens.

7. Share chicken onto serving plates and spoon mushroom sauce over chicken, garnish with parsley. Serve and enjoy!

Chicken Cacciatore

Preparation time: 15 minutes

Cook time: 40 minutes

Total time: 55 minutes

Serves: 5

Ingredients:

- 6 Oz. bone-in chicken thighs, with skin
- 1 Tbsp. olive oil
- 3 stalks celery, chopped
- ½ Onion, chopped (4 oz.) package sliced fresh mushrooms
- Cloves garlic, minced (14 ounce) can stewed tomatoes
- 2 Tsp. herbs de Provence
- ¾ Cup of water cubes chicken bouillon, crumbled
- 2 Tbsp. tomato paste
- 1 Pinch red pepper flakes (optional)
- 1 Pinch ground black pepper to taste (optional)

Cooking Instructions:

1. Rinse chicken thighs and pat dry with paper towels. Heat oil in the Instant Pot using Sauté mode.

2. Add chicken. Cook until browned, about 6 minutes per side. Transfer chicken to a plate, reserving drippings in the pot.

3. Add the celery, onion, and mushrooms in the pot; cook and stir until soft, about 5 minutes. Add garlic; cook until fragrant, about 2 minutes.

4. Add chicken back to the Instant Pot; add tomatoes and tomato paste. Sprinkle with herbs de Provence, water and bouillon.

5. Secure the lid and make sure the valve is set to sealing position. Select Manual High Pressure button to cook for 11 minutes.

6. When timer beeps, use natural pressure release for about 5 minutes, then release any remaining pressure.

7. Unlock and remove lid carefully. Season the chicken to taste with red pepper flakes and black pepper.

8. Serve and enjoy!

Chicken Cordon Bleu

Preparation time: 12 minutes

Cook time: 15 minutes

Total time: 27 minutes

Serves: 5

Ingredients:

- 1 Cup of panko breadcrumbs
- 1 Tsp salt
- ½ Tsp pepper
- 3-4 Chicken breast halves boneless, skinless
- Slices deli ham, thinly sliced
- Slices Swiss cheese
- ½ Cup of butter, melted
- 1 Cup of chicken broth

Cooking Instructions

1. In a shallow dish, combine Panko, salt, and pepper. Set aside.

2. Pound chicken breast to ½" thickness. Place 2 slices of ham over each chicken breast.

3. Place slice of Swiss cheese over the ham and roll chicken up tightly. Dip each chicken roll in butter, roll in breadcrumbs.

4. Place in Instant Pot, seam side down. Pour remaining butter over the chicken and add chicken broth in the cracks between the chicken breasts.

5. Secure the lid and make sure the valve is set to sealing position. Select Manual High Pressure button to cook for 8 minutes.

6. When timer beeps, use natural pressure release for about 5 minutes, then release any remaining pressure.

7. Carefully remove chicken from Instant Pot.

8. Serve and enjoy!

Chicken Chile Verde

Preparation time: 8 minutes

Cook time: 25 minutes

Total time: 33 minutes

Serves: 6

Ingredients:

- Lbs. chicken thighs or chicken breasts
- ½ Tsp. ground cumin
- ¼ Tsp. garlic powder
- 16 Oz. salsa verde
- Salt and black pepper, to taste

Cooking Instructions:

1. Place the chicken in the Instant Pot.

2. Add the cumin, garlic powder, and salsa verde.

3. Cover the lid and make sure the valve is set to sealing position. Select Poultry button to cook for 25 minutes.

4. When timer beeps, use natural pressure release for about 5 minutes, then release any remaining pressure. Shred the chicken in the pot with two forks.

5. Season with salt and black pepper, to taste and top with tortillas, rice, burritos, quesadillas, tacos, salads, etc.

6. Serve and enjoy!

INSTANT POT BEAN & GRAIN RECIPES

Refried Black Beans

Preparation time: 10 minutes

Cook time: 40 minutes

Total time: 50 minutes

Serves: 6

Ingredients:

- 1 Lb. dried black beans (about 2 cups)
- 1 White onion, peeled, halved
- 1 Tbsp. lard or vegetable oil
- 1 ½ Tsp. kosher salt
- 1 Sprig cilantro, plus more for serving
- Grated cotija cheese, chopped radishes, and lime wedges (for serving)

Cooking Instructions:

1. Mix beans, onion, lard, salt, cilantro sprig, and 6 cups of water into Instant Pot.

2. Cover the lid and make sure the valve is set to sealing position. Select Poultry button to cook for 20 minutes.

3. When timer beeps, use natural pressure release for about 10 minutes, then release any remaining pressure.

4. Open the lid and turn the heat to medium or "Sauté." Bring to a strong simmer and mash beans with a potato masher or large wooden spoon.

5. Continue to cook, stirring occasionally, until liquid thickens, about 15 minutes. Taste and season with more salt if necessary.

6. Share beans onto serving plates and top with cheese, cilantro, radishes, and limes.

7. Serve and enjoy!

Spiced Coconut Chicken and Rice

Preparation time: 10 minutes

Cook time: 35 minutes

Total time: 45 minutes

Serves: 6

Ingredients:

- 1 Tbsp. extra-virgin olive oil
- 1 Onion, cut into 1/4-inch slices
- 1 (1-inch) Piece ginger, peeled and cut into ¼ inch slices
- 1 Medium garlic cloves, minced
- 1 Tbsp. curry powder
- 1 Tsp. ground turmeric
- 5 Lb. bone-in, skin-on chicken thighs
- Kosher salt
- Freshly ground black pepper
- 1 (14 oz.) Can light coconut milk
- ½ Cup of water
- 1 1/3 Cups jasmine rice, rinsed
- 2 Tbsp. cilantro leaves plus stems, stems and leaves divided
- 1 ½ Tsp. sugar
- 1 Lime, halved (one half cut into wedges, for serving)

Cooking Instructions:

1. Select Sauté on high heat on the Instant Pot and add the oil.

2. Once hot, add the onion and ginger and sauté for 2 minutes. Add the garlic, curry powder, and turmeric and cook, stirring, for 1 minute.

3. Add the chicken and season with salt and pepper. Add the coconut milk and water. Secure the lid and make sure the valve is set to sealing position.

4. Select Manual High Pressure button to cook for 13 minutes. When timer beeps, use natural pressure release for about 5 minutes, then release any remaining pressure.

5. Transfer the chicken to a platter. Add the rice, chopped cilantro stems, and sugar and secure the lid. Select Manual and cook on high pressure for 4 minutes.

6. Meanwhile, remove the skin and bones from the chicken and discard. When the rice is cooked, use natural pressure release for about 5 minutes, and then release any remaining pressure.

7. Add the chicken back to the pot and add the juice of half the lime. Stir and season with salt and pepper.

8. Share into serving plates and topped with cilantro leaves and lime wedges.

9. Serve and enjoy!

Mexican Rice and Beans

Preparation time: 10 minutes

Cook time: 40 minutes

Total time: 50 minutes

Serves: 7

Calories 275 kcal

Ingredients:

- ½ Tbsp. avocado oil
- 1 Onion diced
- 1 Yellow or red pepper diced
- 1 Tsp. minced garlic
- 2 Cups of short grain brown rice
- 1 Cup of dried red beans
- 1 Cup of salsa
- 1 Tbsp. taco seasoning
- 6 Cups of vegetable or chicken stock
- Cheese, sour cream, cilantro for serving

Cooking Instructions

1. Set Instant Pot to sauté mode on high and allow to heat.

2. Once heated, add oil, onions, and peppers and sauté for about 3 minutes or until it begins to soften.

3. Add garlic and sauté for 1 minute longer. Add rice, beans, salsa, seasonings and stock, and stir.

4. Secure the lid and make sure the valve is set to sealing position. Select Manual High Pressure button to cook for 40 minutes.

5. When timer beeps, use natural pressure release for about 10 minutes, then release any remaining pressure.

6. Serve and enjoy!

New Orleans-Style Red Beans and Rice

Preparation time: 15 minutes

Cook time: 50 minutes

Total time: 1 hour 5 minutes

Serves: 7

Calories 275 kcal

Ingredients:

- 1 Tbsp. oil
- 1 Lb. smoked sausage, sliced
- ¼ Stick of butter
- 2 Cups of chopped seasoning blend (onions, celery, green bell peppers, parsley flakes)
- 1 Clove garlic, chopped
- 1 (1- lb.) Package Camellia Brand Red Kidney Beans
- 2 Cups of water
- 1 Bay leaf
- Salt to taste
- Pepper to taste
- Cajun seasoning to taste
- Hot cooked rice

Cooking Instructions:

1. Rinse and sort beans. Press the Sauté button on the Instant Pot and add oil to it.

2. Add sliced sausage, and sauté for about 5 minutes or until browned. Remove sausage to a paper towel-lined plate and reserve.

3. Add ¼ stick butter to Instant Pot along with chopped seasoning blend, garlic and cook until onions turn soft and clear.

4. Add cooked sausage back to pot along with the beans, water, and bay leaf and stir. Turn Sauté mode off.

5. Secure the lid and make sure the valve is set to sealing position. Select Manual High Pressure button to cook for 40 minutes.

6. When timer beeps, use natural pressure release for about 10 minutes, then release any remaining pressure.

7. Remove lid, and use a spoon or potato masher to mash beans to desired creamy consistency. Add salt, pepper, and Cajun seasoning to taste.

8. Serve with rice and enjoy!

Red Beans and Rice with Sausage

Preparation time: 15 minutes

Cook time: 57 minutes

Total time: 1 hour 12 minutes

Serves: 7

Ingredients:

- ¼ Lb. Bacon (or 2 Tbsp. bacon fat)
- 1 Large Yellow Onion (2 cups diced)
- 4 Stalks Celery, (2 cups diced)
- Cloves Garlic, pressed or minced
- Bay Leaves
- 1 Green Bell Pepper, chopped
- 1 Red Bell Pepper, chopped
- ½ Tsp. Sage, dried
- 1/2 Tsp. Basil, dried
- 1 Tbsp. Cajun / Creole Seasoning (such as Tony Chachere's, or my Cajun Spice Blend) or more to taste
- 4 Cups of Chicken Broth, low sodium
- 1 Lb. Small Red Beans (such as Camellia) sorted & rinsed
- 1 ½ Lbs. Andouille Sausage (or a good smoky Kielbasa) sliced in 3/4" rounds
- ¼ Cup Parsley, chopped
- 2 Cups of Cooked White Rice
- Green Onions, for garnish (optional)
- Hot Sauce, as much as you like!

Cooking Instructions:

1. Set the Instant Pot to Sauté mode. Add the bacon and cook, stirring occasionally until it renders the fat.

2. Remove the bacon and set aside. If using bacon fat, let it heat up and then proceed.

3. If you are using Andouille sausage, add it, sauté to brown on both sides and remove and set aside. If using kielbasa, don't brown it, add it with the beans.

4. Add the onions and celery. Cook for a couple of minutes scraping the bottom of the pot to get the brown bits up. You may add just a splash of the broth to help loosen it.

5. Add the garlic, bay leaves, green and red bell peppers, sage, and basil. Cook, stirring frequently, until onion is translucent. Add the Cajun/Creole seasoning and stir.

6. Add the broth, beans, and sausage stir and secure the lid on the Instant Pot making sure the valve is set to sealing position.

7. Select Manual High Pressure button to cook for 40 minutes. When timer beeps, use natural pressure release for about 10 minutes, then release any remaining pressure.

8. Open the lid. Carefully stir the beans with a long handled spoon. Mash some of the beans and stir to make a more creamy consistency.

9. Taste and add more seasoning if desired. Stir in the chopped parsley. Share into serving plates over cooked white rice and garnish with green onions and hot sauce.

10. Serve and enjoy!

Cherry & Spice Rice Pudding

Preparation time: 9 minutes

Cook time: 13 minutes

Total time: 22 minutes

Serves: 8

Ingredients:

- 1 Cups cooked rice
- 1 Can 12 oz. evaporated milk
- 1 Cup of 2% milk
- 1/3 Cup of sugar
- ¼ Cup of water
- ¾ Cup of dried cherries
- 2 Tbsp. butter, softened
- 2 Tsp. vanilla extract
- ½ Tsp. ground cinnamon
- ¼ Tsp. ground nutmeg

Cooking Instructions:

1. Heat the Instant Pot with oil.

2. Add rice, milks, sugar and water; stir to combine. Stir in remaining ingredients.

3. Secure the lid and make sure the valve is set to sealing position.

4. Select Manual High Pressure button to cook for 4 minutes.

5. When timer beeps, use natural pressure release for about 5 minutes, then release any remaining pressure.

6. Open the lid and stir lightly.

7. Serve and enjoy!

Beans and Brown Rice

Preparation time: 9 minutes

Cook time: 45 minutes

Total time: 54 minutes

Serves: 4

Calories: 477 kcal

Ingredients:

Beans:

- 1 Tbsp. olive oil
- 1 Medium onion
- Garlic cloves
- 15 Oz. can of diced tomatoes, We used the one with herbs
- 1 Tsp. dried oregano
- ½ Tsp. cumin powder
- ½ Tsp. smoked paprika
- ½ Tsp. chipotle powder
- ¼ Tsp. cayenne pepper, optional
- 1 Cup of black beans, 210 grams, soaked in warm water for 2 hours
- 2 Cups of water, 12 oz.
- 1 Tsp. salt, or to taste
- 3 Tbsp. chopped cilantro
- Lime juice

Brown Rice:

- 2 Cups of brown rice, 390 grams
- 2 ½ Cups of water, 20 oz.
- 1 Tsp. oil, optional
- Avocado, To Serve

Cooking Instructions:

1. Soak black beans in warm water for 2 hours. After 2 hours, drain the water and set the beans aside.

2. Press the sauté button on your Instant Pot. Once it displays hot add oil and then add onion and garlic. Cook for 3 minutes until onions are softened.

3. Stir in the can of tomatoes, add cumin powder, smoked paprika, oregano, ¼ tsp. chipotle powder, cayenne pepper (if using). Cook for about 3 minutes or

until tomatoes and spices are well cooked. Add soaked beans, water, salt and mix well. Place a trivet inside the Instant Pot.

4. Place a container (which would fit into the Instant Pot) filled with brown rice on top of the trivet. Add water, oil (optional) to the rice container.

5. Cover the container with lid. Close the pot with its lid. Select Manual High Pressure button to cook for 22 minutes.

6. When timer beeps, use natural pressure release for about 10 minutes, then release any remaining pressure.

7. Open the pot carefully, fluff the rice with a fork and remove the rice container. Remove trivet and then press the sauté button.

8. Mash some of the beans (optional), add cilantro and simmer for 2-3 minutes. Add remaining ¼ tsp. chipotle powder.

9. Adjust spices to taste. Also squeeze in some fresh lime juice. Share to serving plates with avocado slices.

10. Serve and enjoy!

INSTANT POT LAMB, BEEF & PORK RECIPES

Beef and Butternut Squash Stew

Preparation time: 15 minutes

Cook time: 33 minutes

Total time: 48 minutes

Serves: 4

Calories: 287 kcal

Ingredients:

- 1 Large onion, chopped
- 2 Cloves garlic, minced
- 2 Celery stalks, chopped
- 2 Carrots chopped
- 2 Tbsp. tomato paste
- 1 Tomato, peeled and chopped
- 2 Lbs. beef stew cut in 1" pieces
- 1 Tbsp. arrowroot starch
- 4 Cups of peeled and chopped butternut squash cut in 1" cubes
- ½ Cup of Marsala wine
- 2 ½ Cup of beef broth
- 1 Tbsp. extra virgin olive oil
- 2 Bay leaves
- 1 Tsp. sweet Hungarian paprika
- 1 Tsp. thyme
- 1 Tsp. rosemary

Cooking Instructions:

1. Add 1 tbsp. olive oil to the Instant Pot. Add onions, garlic, celery, carrots, tomato and tomato paste to the pot.

2. Season well with salt and freshly ground black pepper and stir. Season beef stew with salt, black pepper and 4 tbsp. of arrowroot starch (or cornstarch).

3. Add beef and butternut squash to the pot. Season butternut squash with salt and freshly ground black pepper.

4. Season everything with sweet Hungarian paprika, thyme, rosemary and add 2 bay leaves. Give everything a good stir.

5   Pour wine and beef broth, and the remaining 2 tbsp. of the olive oil. Secure the lid and make sure the valve is set to sealing position.

6   Select Manual High Pressure button to cook for 30 minutes. When timer beeps, use natural pressure release for about 5 minutes, then release any remaining pressure.

7   Serve and enjoy!

Boneless Pork Chops

Preparation time: 10 minutes

Cook time: 8 minutes

Total time: 18 minutes

Serves: 3

Ingredients:

- 2 Pork chops, boneless 1" thick
- 2 Tbsp. brown sugar
- 1 Tsp. salt
- 1 Tsp. black pepper
- 1 Tsp. paprika
- ½ Tsp. onion powder
- 1 Tbsp. butter
- 1 Cup of chicken broth
- ½ Tbsp. Worcestershire sauce
- 1 Tsp. Liquid Smoke

Cooking Instructions:

1. Mix spices with brown sugar and rub into both sides of pork chops.

2. Set Instant Pot on sauté (high) and add tbsp. butter. Once hot, add pork chops and sauté to brown on both sides for 1-2 minutes each.

3. Remove pork chops and set aside. Add 1 cup of chicken broth and use a wooden spoon to deglaze the bits off the bottom of the pot.

4. Add Worcestershire sauce, liquid smoke and pork chops directly to the Instant Pot in the liquid. Secure the lid, make sure vent is set to sealing position.

7. Select Manual High Pressure button to cook for 8 minutes. When timer beeps, use natural pressure release for about 5 minutes, then release any remaining pressure.

8. Serve and enjoy!

Sticky Hoisin Baby Back Ribs

Preparation time: 5 minutes

Cook time: 25 minutes

Total time: 30 minutes

Serves: 4

Ingredients:

- 4 Lb. baby back pork ribs (about 2 racks)
- 2 Tsp. kosher salt
- 1 Tsp. freshly ground black pepper
- 1/3 Cup hoisin sauce
- 1/3 Cup honey
- 1/3 Cup soy sauce, preferably dark
- 2 Tbsp. Shaoxing rice wine or dry sherry
- 1 Tbsp. finely chopped fresh ginger
- ½ Tsp. five-spice powder
- Flaky sea salt

Cooking Instructions:

1. Cut meat between bones into individual ribs; season with kosher salt and pepper. Let sit at room temperature at least 30 minutes and up to 1 hour.

2. Whisk hoisin, honey, soy sauce, rice wine, ginger, and five-spice powder into the Instant Pot. Toss ribs in sauce to coat, then fit as many as possible in a single layer; set remaining ribs on top.

5. Secure the lid making sure steam release valve is in the proper sealed position. Select Manual High Pressure button to cook for 12 minutes.

6. When timer beeps, use natural pressure release for about 5 minutes, then release any remaining pressure. Open the lid. The ribs should be tender enough to easily pierce with a sharp knife.

7. Transfer ribs to a platter. Select "Sauté" and let cooking liquid simmer until reduced by about half, 10–15 minutes. Preheat your broiler.

8. Brush ribs with sauce. Broil the meat until browned and crisp in places. Flip ribs to platter. Top with sea salt remaining sauce.

9. Serve and enjoy!

Japanese Pork Tender Rib Stew

Preparation time: 10 minutes

Cook time: 45 minutes

Total time: 55 minutes

Serves: 4

Ingredients:

- 820 (gm) Soft pork ribs (pork cartilage)
- Slices ginger
- 1 Clove garlic, minced
- 3 Tbsp. Japanese salt-reduced light soy sauce
- 2 Tbsp. mirin
- 1 Tbsp. cooking rice wine
- 1 Tsp. white vinegar
- ½ Tbsp. rock sugar, roughly pounded
- 1 Cup of water
- 400 (gm) Radish, peeled and roughly chopped
- Salt to taste
- Spring onion, for garnish

Thickening:

- 2 Tsp. corn flour / corn starch
- 1 Tbsp. water

Cooking Instructions:

1. Blanch the pork ribs. Drain well. Set aside.

2. Press Sauté mode on the Instant Pot and sauté oil. Brown the pork ribs on both sides in two batches.

3. Return all the pork ribs into the Instant Pot. Add ginger, garlic, soy sauce, mirin, wine, vinegar, rock sugar and water.

4. Secure the lid making sure steam release valve is in the proper sealed position. Select Manual High Pressure button to cook for 35 minutes.

5. When timer beeps, use natural pressure release for about 5 minutes, then release any remaining pressure.

6. Add the radish. Cover the lid with "sealing" position again. Press "Meat/Stew" and cook for another 10 minutes. Use natural pressure release for about 5 minutes again.

7. Season with salt. Stir in the thickening and cook to your preferred consistency. Garnish with spring onion.

8. Serve enjoy!

BBQ Baby Back Ribs

Preparation time: 10 minutes

Cook time: 30 minutes

Total time: 40 minutes

Serves: 4

Ingredients:

- 1 or 2 Racks baby back ribs, (3 1/2 lbs. total)
- 2 Cups of apple juice
- ½ Cup of cider vinegar
- ½ Cup of favorite barbecue sauce

Cooking Instructions:

1. With a rack bone side up, and starting at one end, slip a knife tip under the membrane, loosening it from the bone.

2. Once you have lifted enough to get a good grip, grasp the membrane with a paper towel and peel it off the rack.

3. Repeat with the remaining rack(s). Cut the rack(s) in half crosswise. Stack the ribs in the Instant Pot. Pour in the apple juice and vinegar.

4. Secure the lid making sure steam release valve is in the proper sealed position. Select the Meat/Stew setting and set the cooking time for 20 minutes at high pressure.

5. When timer beeps, use natural pressure release for about 5 minutes, then release any remaining pressure. Share onto serving plates.

6. Preheat the Instant Pot and line a sheet pan with aluminum foil or a silicone baking mat.

7. Open the Instant Pot and transfer the ribs to the prepared sheet pan using a pair of tongs. Discard the cooking liquid.

8. Brush the ribs on both sides with the barbecue sauce. Bake for about 10 minutes until the sauce is browned. Remove and cut the ribs apart.

9. Serve and enjoy!

Cuban Pulled Pork Sandwiches

Preparation time: 17 minutes

Cook time: 30 minutes

Total time: 47 minutes

Serves: 15

Ingredients:

- 1 Boneless pork shoulder butt roast (4 to 5 pounds)
- 2 Tsp. salt
- 2 Tsp. pepper
- 1 Tbsp. olive oil
- 1 Cup of orange juice
- ½ Cup of lime juice
- Garlic cloves, minced
- 2 Tbsp. spiced rum, optional
- 2 Tbsp. ground coriander
- 2 Tsp. white pepper
- 1 Tsp. cayenne pepper

Sandwiches:

- 2 Loaves (1 lb. each) French bread
- Yellow mustard, optional
- 16 Dill pickle slices
- 1 ½ Lbs. thinly sliced deli ham
- 1 ½ Lbs. Swiss cheese, sliced

Cooking Instructions:

1. Cut pork into 2 thick pieces; season with salt and pepper.

2. Select sauté setting on Instant Pot. Add oil; working in batches, brown pork on all sides.

3. Remove and set aside. Add orange and lime juices, stirring to scrape browned bits from bottom of cooker.

4. Add garlic, rum, if desired, coriander, white pepper and cayenne pepper. Return pork and any collected juices to Instant Pot.

5. Secure the lid making sure steam release valve is in the proper sealed position. Select Manual High Pressure button to cook for 25 minutes.

6. When timer beeps, use natural pressure release for about 10 minutes, then release any remaining pressure.

7. Remove roast; when cool enough to handle, shred with two forks. Remove 1 cup cooking liquid from Instant Pot; add to pork and toss.

8. Cut each loaf of bread in half lengthwise. If desired, spread mustard over cut sides of bread.

9. Layer bottom halves of bread with pickles, pork, ham and cheese. Replace tops. Cut each loaf into eight slices.

10. Serve and enjoy!

Pork Vindaloo

Preparation time: 10 minutes

Cook time: 25 minutes

Total time: 35 minutes

Serves: 6

Ingredients:

- 5 Lbs. (1.44 kg) boneless pork shoulder, cubed
- 1 Tsp. sea salt
- ¼ (60 ml) Cup of olive oil
- 1 Large white onion, peeled and finely chopped
- Cloves garlic, peeled and minced
- 1 Piece fresh ginger, peeled and grated
- 2 Tbsp. vindaloo seasoning or Madras curry
- 1 Tsp. hot paprika
- ½ Tsp. ground turmeric
- 1 Tbsp. all-purpose flour
- ⅓ (80 ml) Cup of Champagne vinegar
- 1 (14 ½ lbs.) Can diced tomatoes in juice
- 1 (250 ml) Cup of reduced-sodium chicken broth

Cooking Instructions:

1. Sprinkle cubed pork with a slat. Heat 2 tablespoons olive oil over medium-high heat on the Instant Pot.

2. Working in batches, brown the meat in a single layer on all sides, 5-7 minutes per batch. Using a slotted spoon, transfer browned pork to a plate.

3. Add chopped white onion and cook, stirring until soft or for about 3 minutes. Stir in garlic, ginger, and spices. Cook stirring for about 30 seconds.

4. Sprinkle all-purpose flour and stir to cook. Return browned pork to Instant Pot. Stir in vinegar, tomatoes with their juice and chicken broth.

5. Mix well, scrapping any browned bits from the bottom of the Instant Pot and boil it. Secure the lid making sure steam release valve is in the proper sealed position.

6. Select Manual High Pressure button to cook for 25 minutes. When timer beeps, use natural pressure release for about 10 minutes, then release any remaining pressure.

7   Remove pot from the heat. Carefully open Instant Pot. Skim any fat from the top of sauce. Sprinkle with fresh chopped cilantro.

8   Serve and enjoy!

Korean Beef

Preparation time: 10 minutes

Cook time: 45 minutes

Total time: 55 minutes

Serves: 6

Ingredients:

- ½ Cup of reduced-sodium soy sauce
- 1/3 Cup of brown sugar packed
- ¼ Cup of reduced-sodium beef broth
- Cloves garlic, minced
- 2 Tbsp. sesame oil
- 2 Tbsp. rice vinegar
- 2 Tbsp. freshly grated ginger
- 3 Tbsp. Gochujang sauce depending on desired heat
- ½ Tsp. onion powder
- ½ Tsp. pepper
- 3-4 Lbs. boneless beef chuck roast cut into 1-inch cubes

Cooking Instructions:

1. In a medium bowl, whisk together first 10 ingredients (up to roast).
2. Place cubed roast into Instant Pot. Pour sauce over cubed meat.
3. Secure the lid making sure steam release valve is in the proper sealed position.
4. Select Meat button to cook for 40 minutes.
5. When timer beeps, use natural pressure release for about 10 minutes, then release any remaining pressure. Share onto serving plates.
6. Serve and enjoy!

Mini Meatballs with Radiatori

Preparation time: 10 minutes

Cook time: 8 minutes

Total time: 18 minutes

Serves: 4

Ingredients:

- 1 Lb. lean ground beef (preferably 93% lean)
- 1 Tbsp. dried basil
- 1 Tsp. dried marjoram
- ½ Tsp. dried thyme
- 2 Tbsp. olive oil
- 1 Large fennel bulb, trimmed and chopped
- 1 Medium yellow onion, chopped
- 1 Medium red bell pepper, stemmed, cored, and chopped
- 30 Oz. dried radiatori
- 1 (28 oz.) Can diced tomatoes (about 3 ½ cups)
- 1 Cup of chicken broth
- ½ Cup of dry white wine, such as Chardonnay
- 1 Tbsp. dried oregano
- ½ Tsp. dried rosemary
- ½ Tsp. grated nutmeg
- ¼ Tsp. salt

Cooking Instructions:

1. Mix the beef, basil, marjoram, and thyme in a medium bowl until the spices are evenly distributed throughout. Form the mixture into twenty 1-inch meatballs.

2. Heat the oil in the Instant Pot, sauté to brown. Add the fennel, onion, and bell pepper; cook, stirring often until the onion turns translucent or about 5 minutes.

3. Stir in the pasta, tomatoes, broth, wine, oregano, rosemary, nutmeg, and salt. Submerge the meatballs in the sauce. Secure the lid making sure steam release valve is in the proper sealed position.

4. Select Manual High Pressure button to cook for 8 minutes. When timer beeps, use natural pressure release for about 10 minutes, then release any remaining pressure.

5. Carefully open the lid and stir. Serve and enjoy!

Pork Chops

Preparation time: 10 minutes

Cook time: 8 minutes

Total time: 18 minutes

Serves: 4

Ingredients:

- Bone-in pork chops
- 1 Tbsp. olive oil
- 1 Tarte apple, peeled, cored and sliced
- 2 Medium shallots, chopped
- 1 Tbsp. chopped fresh thyme
- ½ (125 ml) cup of dry white wine
- ½ (125 ml) cup of reduced-sodium chicken broth
- 1 Tbsp. Dijon mustard
- 1 Tbsp. grainy mustard
- Sea salt and freshly ground black pepper to taste
- 1 Tbsp. crème fraiche (optional)

Cooking Instructions:

1. Season pork chops with salt and black pepper. Heat olive oil on the Instant Pot. Working in a batches, add seasoned pork and brown on both sides.

2. Using a tongs, transfer browned meat to a large plate. Add shallots and apples to the Instant Pot. Cook, stirring until lightly browned. Add thyme, dry white wine and chicken broth.

3. Sauté for sometimes scraping any browned bits from the bottom of pot. Return pork chops to the pot. Secure the lid making sure steam release valve is in the proper sealed position. Select Manual High Pressure button to cook for 8 minutes.

4. When timer beeps, use natural pressure release for about 10 minutes, then release any remaining pressure. Using a tongs, transfer pork chops to a platter. Cover with aluminum foil. Boil cooking liquid in the pot for a few seconds.

5. Stir in mustard and crème fraiche (if using). Remove aluminum foil from pork chops. Pour mustard sauce over share onto serving plates.

6. Serve and enjoy!

Lamb Stew

Preparation time: 15 minutes

Cook time: 35 minutes

Total time: 50 minutes

Serves: 4

Ingredients:

- 2 Lbs. lamb stew meat (you could substitute beef or goat), cut into 1" cubes
- 1 Acorn squash
- Large carrots
- 1 Large yellow onion
- 1 Sprig rosemary (2 if it's small)
- 1 Bay leaf
- Cloves garlic, sliced
- 1 Tbsp. broth or water
- 1 Tsp. salt, to taste (more if using water, less if using broth)

Cooking Instructions:

1. Peel, seed and cube acorn squash. Slice the carrots into thick circles.

2. Peel the onion, cut in half, and then slice into half-moons. Depending on whether you like your veggies softer or firmer in your stew, you can cut the pieces bigger (for firmer) or smaller (for softer).

3. Place all of the ingredients in your Instant Pot. Secure the lid making sure steam release valve is in the proper sealed position.

4. Select Manual High Pressure button to cook for 8 minutes. When timer beeps, use natural pressure release for about 10 minutes, then release any remaining pressure.

5. Carefully remove the lid and give everything a good stir.

6. Serve and enjoy!

Hearty Beef Stew

Preparation time: 10 minutes

Cook time: 35 minutes

Total time: 45 minutes

Serves: 5

Ingredients:

- 1 Lb. stew meat
- 2 Cups of Beef Stock
- 1 Onion (chopped)
- Yukon gold potatoes (chopped)
- 1 Cup of Carrots (chopped)
- 1 Tbsp. Oil (I used olive oil)
- Salt and Pepper to taste
- 1 Tsp. garlic powder
- 1 Tsp. paprika
- 2 Tbsp. flour
- 1 Tbsp. tomato paste

Cooking Instructions:

1. Turn your Instant Pot onto the "Sauté" setting and add your oil and stew meat.

2. Sauté until the meat is no longer pink and then add chopped vegetables. Stir to combine.

3. Add in your broth and seasonings. Stir again. Secure the lid making sure steam release valve is in the proper sealed position.

4. Select "Stew/Meat" button to cook for 35 minutes. When timer beeps, use natural pressure release for about 10 minutes, then release any remaining pressure.

5. Ladle out ¼ of your liquid and combine it with your flour to make it slurry. Add your slurry back into your stew and stir to combine.

6. Add in your salt and pepper to taste.

7. Serve and enjoy!

INSTANT POT EGG RECIPES

Poached Eggs

Preparation time: 5 minutes

Cook time: 2 minutes

Total time: 7 minutes

Serves: 5

Calories: 75 kcal

Ingredients:

- Large eggs
- 1 Cup of water

Cooking Instructions:

1. Place the trivet in the bottom of the Instant Pot liner and pour in 1 cup of water.

2. Spray each silicone cup with Pam cooking spray or rub with ghee.

3. Crack each egg and pour it into the prepared cup. Place the silicone cups into the Instant Pot.

4. Secure the lid making sure steam release valve is in the proper sealed position.

5. Select "Steam" button to cook for 7 minutes.

6. When timer beeps, use natural pressure release for about 10 minutes, then release any remaining pressure.

7. Remove the silicone cups from the liner.

8. Serve and enjoy!

Bacon Cheddar Egg Casserole

Preparation time: 15 minutes

Cook time: 23 minutes

Total time: 38 minutes

Serves: 5

Ingredients:

- Eggs
- ½ Cup half and half
- ½ Tsp. salt
- ¼ Tsp. pepper
- 1 Cup of frozen hash browns
- Salt and pepper
- 2 Handfuls of spinach
- ½ Cup of bacon bits
- 1 Cup of grated cheddar cheese

Cooking Instructions:

1. In a bowl whisk together the eggs and the half and half. Add in ½ tsp. salt and ¼ tsp. pepper. Set aside.

2. Spray an oven safe dish that will fit inside your Instant Pot with non-stick cooking spray. Layer the hash browns in the bottom of the pan.

3. Lightly salt and pepper the hash browns. Then layer on the spinach, bacon bits and finally the cheddar. Pour the egg mixture over the top of everything.

4. Pour 1 cup of water in the bottom of your Instant Pot. Place a trivet in the bottom of the Instant Pot. Cover your casserole pan loosely with foil.

5. Use a foil sling or silicone sling to lower the pan into the Instant Pot, on top of the trivet. Secure the lid making sure steam release valve is in the proper sealed position.

6. Select Manual High Pressure button to cook for 22 minutes. When timer beeps, use natural pressure release for about 10 minutes, then release any remaining pressure.

7. Open the pot and carefully use the sling to remove the pan. Remove the foil. Cut the casserole. Serve and enjoy!

Eggy Muffins

Preparation time: 7 minutes

Cook time: 6 minutes

Total time: 13 minutes

Serves: 2

Ingredients:

- 1 Egg
- Cherry tomatoes, halved
- 1 Tbsp. shredded cheddar cheese
- Salt and pepper to taste

Cooking Instructions:

1. Lightly grease a small ramekin with cooking spray then crack egg into the dish.

2. Top with cherry tomatoes, cheese, and salt and pepper to taste. Pour 1 cup of water into the pressure cooker then lower your trivet into the Instant Pot.

3. Place ramekin on top of trivet. Secure the lid making sure steam release valve is in the proper sealed position.

4. Select Manual High Pressure button to cook for 4 minutes. When timer beeps, use natural pressure release for about 10 minutes, then release any remaining pressure.

5. Serve and enjoy!

Sous Vide Egg Bites

Preparation time: 7 minutes

Cook time: 10 minutes

Total time: 17 minutes

Serves: 4

Ingredients:

- Eggs
- ½ Cups of Monterey jack cheese shredded
- ½ Cup of cottage cheese
- 1 Green onion chopped
- ½ Roasted red pepper chopped
- ¼ Cup of spinach chopped

Cooking Instructions:

1. Add 1 cup of water to Instant Pot and place the trivet inside.

2. Add eggs, Monterey jack, and cottage cheese to a blender and process until smooth (about 30 seconds). Add green onion, red pepper.

3. Give everything a quick stir to combine. Equally divide the egg mixture between the compartments of the silicone mold, tightly cover with aluminum foil.

4. Lower the silicone mold into the Instant Pot. Secure the lid making sure steam release valve is in the proper sealed position.

5. Select Steam button to cook for 10 minutes. When timer beeps, use natural pressure release for about 10 minutes, then release any remaining pressure.

6. Remove the silicone mold from the Instant Pot and allow the egg bites to cool for a few minutes.

7. Serve and enjoy!

Sriracha and Red Pepper Deviled Eggs

Preparation time: 10minutes

Cook time: 5 minutes

Total time: 15 minutes

Serves: 12 deviled eggs

Ingredients:

- Hard-boiled eggs, peeled
- 1 Tbsp. sour cream
- 1 Tbsp. Sriracha sauce
- 1 Tsp. freshly squeezed lime juice
- ¼ Cup very finely diced red bell pepper
- 1 Tsp. paprika

Cooking Instructions:

1. Cut the eggs in half and place the yolks in a mixing bowl.

2. Add the sour cream, Sriracha sauce and lime juice. Mix everything together until the mixture is smooth and creamy.

3. Add the diced bell pepper and stir to combine. Spoon the mixture into the egg whites.

4. Garnish with a sprinkle of paprika over each deviled egg.

5. Serve and enjoy!

Egg Pudding

Preparation time: 10minutes

Cook time: 10 minutes

Total time: 20 minutes

Serves: 4

Ingredients:

- Liquid caramel
- Eggs
- 1 Tbsp. sugar
- 500 Milliliters milk

Cooking Instructions:

1. Spread liquid caramel in a pudding mold with a cover.

2. Place eggs, sugar and milk in a bowl and mix well with an electric mixer. Pour mixture into mold and seal.

3. Place pudding mold in Instant Pot and add water until container is half submerged. Secure the lid making sure steam release valve is in the proper sealed position.

4. Select Manual High Pressure button to cook for 4 minutes. When timer beeps, use natural pressure release for about 10 minutes, then release any remaining pressure.

5. Remove pudding from pan. Share onto serving plates.

6. Serve and enjoy!

Cheesy Egg Bake

Preparation time: 6 minutes

Cook time: 20 minutes

Total time: 26 minutes

Serves: 4

Ingredients:

- Slices bacon, chopped
- 2 Cups of frozen hash browns
- Eggs
- ¼ Cup of milk
- ½ Cup of shredded cheddar cheese
- 1 Tsp. kosher salt
- ½ Tsp. pepper

Optional Toppings:

- Onion, red pepper, spinach, mushrooms, green onions

Cooking Instructions:

1. Chop up bacon into small pieces then sauté in Instant Pot until crispy.

2. Add any extra veggies that you would like and sauté until tender or about 3 minutes. Add in frozen hash browns and stir until slightly thawed or about 2 minutes.

3. Grease a heat proof container that will fit into your Instant Pot. Whisk together eggs, milk, shredded cheese, and salt and pepper in a separate bowl.

4. Add bacon and veggie mixture to the eggs. Pour the egg mixture into your greased, heat proof container. Pour 1 ½ cups of water into Instant Pot and set trivet inside.

5. Place heat proof bowl with egg mixture on top of trivet. Secure the lid making sure steam release valve is in the proper sealed position.

6. Select Manual High Pressure button to cook for 20 minutes. When timer beeps, use natural pressure release for about 10 minutes, then release any remaining pressure.

7. Loosen edges then dump out onto large plate, top with green onions and extra shredded cheese. Serve and enjoy!

Chinese Savory Steamed Egg

Preparation time: 6 minutes

Cook time: 10 minutes

Total time: 16 minutes

Serves: 2

Ingredients:

- 2 Large eggs
- 175 Ml ¾ cup of warm water
- ½ Tsp. salt
- ⅓ Tsp. sesame oil
- Soy sauce to taste
- Scallions for garnish

Cooking Instructions:

1. Beat the egg with ½ tsp. salt in a bowl until the egg is well beaten.

2. Heat the water for about 45 seconds. Add the water while stirring the egg in one direction.

3. Pour the egg mixture through a strainer to remove the foam. Cover the bowl with foil. Add 2 cups of water to Instant Pot.

4. Secure the lid making sure steam release valve is in the proper sealed position. Select "Steam" setting to cook for 5 minutes.

5. When timer beeps, use natural pressure release for about 10 minutes, then release any remaining pressure.

6. Serve and enjoy!

Hard Boiled Eggs

Preparation time: 6 minutes

Cook time: 6 minutes

Total time: 12 minutes

Serves: 4

Ingredients:

- Eggs
- 1 Cup of water

Cooking Instructions:

1. Place the steamer basket in the Instant Pot. Add the water and the eggs.

2. Secure the lid making sure steam release valve is in the proper sealed position. Select Manual High Pressure to cook for 5 minutes.

3. When timer beeps, use natural pressure release for about 8 minutes, then release any remaining pressure.

4. Open the lid. Remove the steamer basket from the Instant Pot. Put eggs into ice cold water to cool.

5. You can put the eggs on a rack or trivet as well, but I prefer the basket so the eggs are easier to remove from the pressure cooking pot.

6. You can cook a single egg or as many as will fit in your steamer basket and the cook time will be the same.

7. Serve and enjoy!

Quick Egg Custard

Preparation time: 6 minutes

Cook time: 7 minutes

Total time: 13 minutes

Serves: 6

Ingredients:

- 2 Cups Milk 1%, 2% or Whole
- Large Eggs
- ¾ Cup of White Sugar
- 1 Tsp. Vanilla Extract optional
- A pinch Sea Salt
- ¼ Tsp Ground Cinnamon optional
- Stack N' Cook Pressure Cooker Insert Pans

Garnish:

- Nutmeg freshly grated
- Fresh Fruit
- Ground Cinnamon

Cooking Instructions:

1. In a medium bowl, beat eggs. Add milk, sugar, salt and vanilla and blend until combined.

2. Pour into Instant Pot safe bowl and cover with foil or lid. Add ½ cup of water to Instant Pot and place trivet in bottom.

3. Place bowl on top of trivet. Secure the lid making sure steam release valve is in the proper sealed position. Select Manual High Pressure to cook for 7 minutes.

4. When timer beeps, use natural pressure release for about 10 minutes, then release any remaining pressure.

5. Top with a dusting of nutmeg, berries or other fruit, if desired.

6. Serve and enjoy!

French "Baked" Eggs

Preparation time: 6 minutes

Cook time: 8 minutes

Total time: 14 minutes

Serves: 4

Ingredients:

- Eggs
- Slices of Meat, Fish or Vegetables
- Slices of Cheese, or shot of cream
- Garnish of Fresh Herbs
- Olive Oil

Cooking Instructions:

1. Add one cup of water to the Instant Pot and set aside.

2. Prepare the ramekins by adding a drop of olive oil in each and rubbing the bottom and sides. Then, lay a slice of preferred meat or vegetable.

3. Break an egg and drop it into the ramekin. Add sliced cheese, or cream of choice. For a soft egg yolk, cover tightly with tin foil.

4. For a hard fully cooked yolk, leave uncovered. Place ramekins in the steamer basket and lower into Instant Pot.

5. Secure the lid making sure steam release valve is in the proper sealed position. Select Manual Low Pressure to cook for 5 minutes.

6. When timer beeps, use natural pressure release for about 8 minutes, then release any remaining pressure.

7. Serve and enjoy!

Artichoke and Asparagus Deviled Eggs

Preparation time: 10 minutes

Cook time: 7 minutes

Total time: 17 minutes

Serves: 12 deviled eggs

Ingredients:

- Hard-boiled eggs, peeled
- ¼ Cup of steamed asparagus, chopped
- 1 Tbsp. sour cream
- 1 Tbsp. mayonnaise
- 1 Tbsp. fresh parsley, chopped
- 1 Tsp. mustard
- 1 Tsp. freshly squeezed lemon juice
- ¼ Cup very finely diced marinated artichoke hearts
- ¼ Tsp. fine sea salt

Cooking Instructions:

1. Cut the eggs in half and place the yolks in a mixing bowl.

2. Add the asparagus, sour cream, mayonnaise, and parsley, mustard and lemon juice.

3. Using a hand blender, blend the mixture until smooth. Add the finely diced artichoke hearts and stir to combine. Add the sea salt to taste.

4. Spoon the mixture into the egg whites. Garnish with very small tips of asparagus, a sprinkling of parsley and, if desired, a bit of fresh lemon zest.

5. Serve and enjoy!

INSTANT POT VEGAN RECIPES

Vegan Cauliflower Queso

Preparation time: 10 minutes

Cook time: 5 minutes

Total time: 15 minutes

Serves: 4

Ingredients:

- 2 Cups of cauliflower florets (about 1/2 head small cauliflower)
- 1 Cup of water
- ¾ Cup of thick-cut carrot coins
- ¼ Cup of raw cashews
- ¼ Cup of nutritional yeast
- Liquid drained from 1 (10-oz.) can diced tomatoes with green chilies
- ½ Tsp. smoked paprika
- ½ Tsp. salt (or to taste)
- ¼ Tsp. chili powder
- ¼ Tsp. jalapeño powder, optional
- 1/8 Tsp. mustard powder

Optional Toppings:

- 1 10 Oz. can diced tomatoes with green chilies, drained (I like Rotel)
- ½ Cup of chopped bell pepper
- 2 Tbsp. minced red onion
- ¼ Cup of minced cilantro

Cooking Instructions:

1. Add the cauliflower, water, carrots and cashews to your Instant Pot.

2. Secure the lid making sure steam release valve is in the proper sealed position. Select Manual High Pressure to cook for 5 minutes.

3. When timer beeps, use natural pressure release for about 8 minutes, then release any remaining pressure.

4. Pour the cooked mixture into a strainer over the sink and drain the extra water.

5. Using a blender, put the drained mixture along with the nutritional yeast, liquid drained from the canned tomatoes, smoked paprika, salt, chili powder, jalapeño powder (if using) and mustard powder into your blender.

6. Blend until smooth. Scrape out the blender contents into a mixing bowl and stir in the tomatoes and green chilies, bell pepper (if using), minced onion (if using) and cilantro.

7. Serve and enjoy!

Lentil Curry

Preparation time: 10 minutes

Cook time: 6 minutes

Total time: 16 minutes

Serves: 5

Ingredients:

- 1 ½ Cups green or brown lentils
- ½ Tbsp. coconut oil
- 1 Small shallot, finely chopped
- 1 Tbsp. minced fresh ginger
- 2 Tbsp. minced garlic (about 6 cloves)
- 1 Tbsp. plus 1 teaspoon curry powder
- ½ Tbsp. coconut sugar or brown sugar
- 1 Tsp. kosher salt
- ¾ Tsp. ground turmeric
- ¼ Tsp. cayenne pepper (use more for more spice or omit if sensitive to spice)
- 1 14 Oz. can light coconut milk
- 2 Tbsp. freshly squeezed lemon juice (about 1/2 large lemon)
- Cooked brown rice, for serving
- Chopped fresh cilantro, for serving

Cooking Instructions:

1. Rinse and drain the lentils, then set aside. Set the Instant Pot to sauté and add the coconut oil.

2. Once the oil has melted, add 1 tbsp. of water, shallot, ginger, and garlic. Cook, stirring often, until very fragrant and the shallot is soft.

3. Add the curry powder, coconut sugar, salt, turmeric, and cayenne and stir. Add the lentils, coconut milk, and 1 cup of water. Stir to coat the lentils completely with the liquid.

4. Secure the lid making sure steam release valve is in the proper sealed position. Select Manual High Pressure to cook for 15 minutes. When timer beeps, use natural pressure release for about 10 minutes, then release any remaining pressure.

5. Open the lid and stir in the lemon juice. Taste and adjust the seasoning as desired. If the curry is too thick, add a bit more water to loosen as needed. Serve with rice and sprinkle cilantro.

Vegan Potato Curry

Preparation time: 10 minutes

Cook time: 40 minutes

Total time: 50 minutes

Serves: 5

Ingredients:

- 1 Medium yellow onion , chopped
- Large cloves of garlic, chopped finely
- 900g Or about 5 heaping cups of baby potatoes
- 2 Tbsp. curry powder or curry paste
- 500mls/ Around 2 cups of water
- 400g / 2 Heaping cups of fresh green beans , chopped into bite sized pieces
- 1 400ml Can coconut milk , full fat or light
- 1 Tbsp. sugar (optional)
- Salt & pepper to taste
- 1 Tsp. chili pepper flakes or a small fresh chili chopped (optional)
- 1 Tbsp. arrowroot powder , or corn starch

Cooking Instructions:

1. Set your instant pot to sauté. Once hot, add a few drops of water and cook the onions until soft.

2. Add the garlic and cook for one minute longer. Add everything else to the Instant Pot except the green beans and arrowroot/cornstarch.

3. Secure the lid making sure steam release valve is in the proper sealed position. Select Manual High Pressure to cook for 20 minutes.

4. When timer beeps, use natural pressure release for about 10 minutes, then release any remaining pressure. Carefully remove the lid.

5. Add the arrowroot/cornstarch into a small bowl or cup and mix into it a few tbsp. of water to make it thick and slurry. Pour it into the Instant Pot stirring as you go.

6. Add salt and pepper to taste then add the green beans and cook for about 5 minutes or until they are tendered and the gravy has thickened.

7. Serve and enjoy!

Vegan Lentil Chili

Preparation time: 8 minutes

Cook time: 5 minutes

Total time: 13 minutes

Serves: 6

Ingredients:

- 1 Tbsp. olive oil
- 1 Onion, chopped
- Cloves minced garlic
- 2 Carrots, chopped
- 1-2 Jalapeños, chopped
- 1 ½ Tbsp. chili powder
- 1 Tbsp. cumin
- ½ Tbsp. ground coriander
- 1 Tbsp. dried oregano
- 1 ½ Tbsp. salt
- 1 15 Oz. can crushed tomatoes
- 1 28 oz. can fire roasted diced tomatoes
- 2 Cups of brown or green lentils cups of vegetable broth
- 1 Tsp. fresh lime juice
- ½ Cup of chopped fresh cilantro

Cooking Instructions:

1. Press the sauté button on the Instant Pot.

2. Heat the olive oil in the pot, then add the onion, garlic, carrots and jalapeños and sauté for about 3-4 minutes or until soft.

3. Add the spices and remaining ingredients except for lime juice and cilantro, then cover. Secure the lid making sure steam release valve is in the proper sealed position.

4. Select Manual High Pressure to cook for 20 minutes. When timer beeps, use natural pressure release for about 10 minutes, then release any remaining pressure.

5. Stir in lime juice and cilantro.

6. Serve and enjoy

Easy Jackfruit Curry

Preparation time: 15 minutes

Cook time: 46 minutes

Total time: 1 hour 1 minute

Serves: 2

Calories: 369 kcal

Ingredients:

- 1 Tsp. oil
- ½ Tsp. cumin seeds
- ½ Tsp. mustard seeds
- ½ Tsp. nigella seeds
- Bay leaves
- 2 Dried red chilies
- 1 Small onion, chopped
- Cloves of garlic, chopped
- 1 Inch ginger, chopped
- 1 Tsp. coriander powder
- ½ Tsp. turmeric
- ¼ Tsp. black pepper
- 2 Medium tomatoes pureed or 1.5 cups puree
- 1 20 Oz. can green Jackfruit drained and rinsed
- ½ Tsp. salt or to taste
- 1 Cups of water

Cooking Instructions:

1. Heat oil in the Instant Pot. When hot, add cumin, mustard and nigella seeds and sauté for 1 minute.

2. Add bay leaves and red chilies and cook for a few seconds. Add in the onion, garlic and ginger and a pinch of salt.

3. Cook for about 5 to 6 minutes or until it softens. Stir occasionally. Add coriander, turmeric, black pepper and mix well. Add pureed tomato, salt and Jackfruit. Mix.

4. Secure the lid making sure steam release valve is in the proper sealed position. Select Manual High Pressure to cook for 15 minutes.

5. When timer beeps, use natural pressure release for about 10 minutes, then release any remaining pressure.

6   Add water, cover and cook for another 15 minutes. Taste and adjust salt and spice.

7   Reduce heat to medium low and cover and cook for another 10 minutes or longer until desired consistency. Garnish with cilantro.

8   Serve and enjoy!

Maple Bourbon Sweet Potato Chili

Preparation time: 15 minutes

Cook time: 15 minutes

Total time: 30 minute

Serves: 5

Calories: 269 kcal

Ingredients:

- 1 Tbsp. cooking oil
- 1 Small yellow onion, thinly sliced
- 2-3 Cloves garlic minced
- 2 Cups of sweet potatoes, peeled and cubed into 1/2" pieces
- 2 Cups of vegetable broth
- 1 ½ Tbsp. chili powder
- 2 Tsp. cumin
- ½ Tsp. paprika
- ¼ Tsp. cayenne pepper
- 2 15 Oz. cans kidney beans, drained and rinsed
- 1 15 Oz. can diced tomatoes
- ¼ Cup of bourbon
- 2 Tbsp. maple syrup
- Salt and pepper, to taste
- A few fresh springs of cilantro
- 2 Green onions, diced
- Small corn tortillas, toasted and sliced (optional)

Cooking Instructions:

1. Turn Instant Pot to sauté, add oil, and let it heat up for 30 seconds.

2. Once oil is hot, add onions and sauté for about 5 minutes, stirring occasionally until onions are softened. Add garlic and sauté for another 30 seconds.

3. Add cubed sweet potatoes, chili powder, cumin, paprika, and cayenne pepper, stirring until vegetables are well coated.

4. Add vegetable broth, beans, tomatoes, maple syrup, and bourbon. Secure the lid making sure steam release valve is in the proper sealed position.

5. Select Manual High Pressure to cook for 15 minutes. When timer beeps, use natural pressure release for about 10 minutes, then release any remaining pressure.

6 Remove lid and check to make sure the sweet potatoes are tendered. If using tortillas, lightly oil a cast iron skillet and pan fry the tortillas on each side for 2-3 minutes or until crispy.

7 Remove from heat and let cool before cutting into thin strips. Serve with cilantro, green onions, and toasted tortillas.

8 Serve and enjoy!

Green Chile Stew

Preparation time: 15 minutes

Cook time: 35 minutes

Total time: 50 minute

Serves: 10 -12 bowls

Ingredients:

Meat:

- ½ Package of Butler Soy Curls rehydrated
- 1 Tsp. Chili Powder
- 1 Tsp. Ground Cumin
- 1 Tsp. Garlic Powder
- 1 Tsp. Onion Powder
- The Broth
- 1 Yellow Onion, diced
- Carrots, diced
- 2 Stalks Celery, diced
- 4-5 Cloves Garlic
- 2 Cups of Vegetable Broth
- 2 Cups of Water
- 1 Tsp. Oregano
- 1 Cup of dried rinsed, Pinto Beans

Stew:

- Yukon Gold Potatoes, cubed
- 15 Oz Can Fire Roasted Tomatoes
- 24 Oz package Select New Mexico Green Chiles
- ¼ Cup of Lime Juice
- ¼ Tsp. Salt
- ¼ Tsp. Ground Pepper

Cooking Instructions:

1. Sauce your 'meat' of choice using the Sauté mode on your Instant Pot.

2. Add the Garlic Powder, Onion Powder, Chili Powder, & Cumin and stir frequently until lightly browned. Use a little veggie broth to keep it from sticking.

3. Remove from pot and set aside. Sauté onion, carrots, and celery on Sauté mode until they are soft and translucent.

4. Deglaze any browned bits on bottom of pot as these add to the flavor. Add minced garlic and stir for 1 minute. Turn off Instant Pot.

5. Add Veggie Broth, Water, Oregano, and dried Beans. Secure the lid making sure steam release valve is in the proper sealed position.

6. Select Manual High Pressure to cook for 35 minutes. When timer beeps, use natural pressure release for about 10 minutes, then release any remaining pressure.

7. Stir broth and add potatoes, chilies, tomatoes, and the "meat" you set aside. Secure the lid and select Manual High Pressure to cook for 8 minutes.

8. When timer beeps, use natural pressure release for about 5 minutes, then release any remaining pressure.

9. Stir in Lime Juice, masa flour - 1 Tbsp. at a time until desired thickness.

10. Serve and enjoy!

Easy Vegan Mashed Potatoes

Preparation time: 10 minutes

Cook time: 20 minutes

Total time: 30 minute

Serves: 5

Calories: 88 kcal

Ingredients:

- 6 Potatoes cubed into large pieces Yukon gold or baking potatoes, peeled if desired.
- Cloves of garlic
- ½ Tsp. salt
- 1 Tbsp. extra virgin olive oil or vegan butter
- A good dash of black pepper
- Dash of parsley or thyme
- Pinch of nutmeg
- 1 Cup of full fat coconut milk
- Fresh chives for garnish

Cooking Instructions:

1. Add the cubed potatoes, garlic cloves, ¼ tsp. salt with ½ cups of water into Instant Pot.

2. Secure the lid making sure steam release valve is in the proper sealed position. Select Manual High Pressure to cook for 5 minutes.

3. When timer beeps, use natural pressure release for about 7 minutes, then release any remaining pressure. Add the potatoes into a large pot, adding enough water to cover them.

4. Bring to a boil and simmer for 10-15 minutes or until they're tendered. Turn into a colander to drain. Transfer to a bowl and allow for few minutes to dry out.

5. Mash lightly and let sit for a minute for the steam to escape. Make sure to mash the cooked garlic. Mix in salt, the rest of the ingredients and half cup coconut milk.

6. Mix and whip lightly, just enough to add air and still have some texture. Keep for a minute for the milks to incorporate and absorb.

7. Taste and adjust. Add ¼ tsp. or more salt as needed. Add more coconut milk for creamier consistency to preference if needed and mix in.

8. Add 1-2 tbsp. nutritional yeast for cheesy potatoes. Garnish with chives.

9. Serve and enjoy!

Vegan Butter Chicken

Preparation time: 12 minutes

Cook time: 30 minutes

Total time: 42 minute

Serves: 4

Calories: 279 kcal

Ingredients:

- Large ripe tomatoes or 1 15 oz. can diced tomatoes
- Cloves of garlic
- ½ inch cube of ginger
- 1 Hot or mild green Chile , I use serrano
- ¾ Cup water , use 1 cup if the tomatoes are not very juicy
- 1 Tsp. garam masala
- ½ Tsp. paprika or Kashmiri chili powder
- ½ Tsp. cayenne
- ¾ Tsp. salt
- 1 Cup of soy curls (dry, not rehydrated)
- 1 Cup of cooked chickpeas
- Cashew cream made with ¼ cup of soaked cashews blended with ½ cup water
- ½ Tsp. or more garam masala
- ½ Tsp. or more sugar or sweetener
- 1 Tsp. kasoori methi - dried fenugreek leaves or add a 1/4 tsp ground mustard
- ½ Moderately hot green chili finely chopped, or use 2 tbsp. finely chopped green bell pepper
- ½ Tsp. minced or finely chopped ginger
- ¼ Cup of cilantro for garnish

Cooking Instructions:

1. Blend the tomatoes, garlic, ginger, chili with water until smooth.

2. Add pureed tomato mixture to the Instant Pot. Add soy curls, chickpeas, spices and salt. Secure the lid making sure steam release valve is in the proper sealed position.

3. Select Manual High Pressure to cook for 10 minutes. When timer beeps, use natural pressure release for about 10 minutes, then release any remaining pressure.

4. Using sauté mode, add the cashew cream, garam masala, sweetener and fenugreek leaves and mix in. Bring to a boil, taste and adjust salt, heat, sweet.

5. Add more cayenne and salt if needed. Fold in the chopped green chili, ginger and cilantro and press cancel.

6. At this point, you can add some vegan butter or oil for additional buttery flavor. Share onto serving plates.

7. Serve and enjoy!

INSTANT POT APPETIZER RECIPES

Homemade Peaches and Cream Oatmeal

Preparation time: 10 minutes

Cook time: 10 minutes

Total time: 20 minutes

Serves: 6

Ingredients:

- 2 Cups of Old Fashioned Oats
- ½ Cup of water
- ½ Cup of milk
- 1 Tsp. salt
- 1 Tsp. ground cinnamon
- ⅓ Cup of sugar
- Peaches

Cooking Instructions:

1. Prepare the peaches by washing, peeling, and chopping.

2. Save a few slices back for garnish. Add all ingredients to Instant Pot and stir together.

3. Secure the lid making sure steam release valve is in the proper sealed position. Select Manual High Pressure to cook for 7 minutes.

4. When timer beeps, use natural pressure release for about 10 minutes, then release any remaining pressure.

5. Share onto serving plates and top with sugar, brown sugar, milk, cream, and extra sliced peaches.

6. Serve and enjoy!

Cocktail Meatballs

Preparation time: 3 minutes

Cook time: 8 minutes

Total time: 11 minute

Serves: 64 pieces

Ingredients:

- 35 Lbs. Cooked Perfect Homestyle Meatballs
- ¼ Cup of brown sugar
- ¼ Cup of honey
- ½ Cup of ketchup
- 1 Tbsp. soy sauce
- 1 Tbsp. minced garlic
- Garnish with sliced green onions (optional)

Cooking Instructions:

1. Combine brown sugar, honey, ketchup, soy sauce, and garlic into Instant Pot.

2. Set to sauté mode and stir to combine. Once the mixture comes to a boil, add the frozen fully cooked meatballs.

3. Secure the lid making sure steam release valve is in the proper sealed position.

4. Select Manual High Pressure to cook for 7 minutes.

5. When timer beeps, use natural pressure release for about 10 minutes, then release any remaining pressure.

6. Serve and enjoy!

Buffalo Ranch Chicken Dip

Preparation time: 3 minutes

Cook time: 15 minutes

Total time: 18 minute

Serves: 6

Ingredients:

- 1 Lb. chicken breast
- 1 Packet ranch dip
- 1 Cup of Hot Sauce
- 1 Stick butter
- 16 Oz. cheddar cheese
- 15 Oz. cream cheese

Cooking Instructions:

1. Add the chicken, cream cheese, butter, hot sauce, and a packet of Ranch dip in your Instant Pot.

2. Secure the lid making sure steam release valve is in the proper sealed position.

3. Select Manual High Pressure to cook for 15 minutes.

4. When timer beeps, use natural pressure release for about 10 minutes, then release any remaining pressure.

5. Shred chicken with fork or use your mixer to break it up. Stir in cheddar cheese. Share onto serving plates with chips.

6. Serve and enjoy!

Beer-Braised Pulled Ham

Preparation time: 10 minutes

Cook time: 25 minutes

Total time: 35 minute

Serves: 15

Ingredients:

- Bottles (12 ounces each) beer or nonalcoholic beer
- ¾ Cup German or Dijon mustard, divided
- ½ Tsp. coarsely ground pepper
- 1 Fully cooked bone-in ham (4 pounds)
- Fresh rosemary sprigs
- 16 Pretzel hamburger buns, split
- Dill pickle slices, optional

Cooking Instructions:

1. Whisk together beer, ½ cup of mustard and pepper into Instant Pot.

2. Add ham and rosemary. Secure the lid making sure steam release valve is in the proper sealed position.

3. Select Manual High Pressure to cook for 20 minutes. When timer beeps, use natural pressure release for about 10 minutes, then release any remaining pressure.

4. Remove ham; cool slightly. Discard rosemary sprigs. Skim fat from liquid remaining in the Instant Pot. Select sauté setting and adjust for high heat.

5. Bring liquid to a boil; cook for 5 minutes. When ham is cool enough to handle, shred meat with two forks. Discard the bone.

6. Place shredded ham on pretzel bun bottoms with remaining mustard and, if desired, dill pickle slices. Replace tops.

7. Serve and enjoy!

Cranberry Pecan Brie

Preparation time: 10 minutes

Cook time: 15 minutes

Total time: 25 minute

Serves: 5

Ingredients:

- 1 (8 oz.) Round of Brie
- ¼ Cup of cranberry jalapeno preserves
- 1 Tbsp. candied pecans
- 1 Tsp. minced fresh thyme

Cooking Instructions:

1. Slice through the rind on top of the Brie in a grid pattern.

2. Add the Brie in a baking dish that will fit in your Instant Pot. Cover baking dish tightly with foil.

3. Prepare a foil sling for lifting the baking dish out of the Instant Pot by taking an 18" strip of foil and folding it twice lengthwise.

4. Pour 1 cup of water into the Instant Pot and place the rack in the bottom. Carefully center the baking dish on the foil strip and lower it into the Instant Pot on to the rack.

5. Fold the foil strips down so that they do not interfere with closing the lid. Secure the lid making sure steam release valve is in the proper sealed position.

6. Select Manual High Pressure to cook for 15 minutes. When timer beeps, use natural pressure release for about 10 minutes, then release any remaining pressure.

7. Check to make sure cheese is melted and piping hot. Remove to a serving plate and top with preserves, pecans and thyme.

8. Serve and enjoy!

Prosciutto-wrapped Asparagus Canes

Preparation time: 6 minutes

Cook time: 8 minutes

Total time: 14 minutes

Serves: 5

Ingredients:

- 1 Lb.(500g) thick Asparagus
- 8 Oz.(225g) thinly sliced Prosciutto

Cooking Instructions:

1. Pour 2 cups of water into the Instant Pot and set aside.

2. Wrap the asparagus spears in prosciutto. Lay any extra un-wrapped spears in a single layer along the bottom of the steamer basket.

3. Place the prosciutto-wrapped asparagus on top in a single layer. Place the basket inside the Instant Pot.

4. Secure the lid making sure steam release valve is in the proper sealed position. Select Manual High Pressure to cook for 4 minutes.

5. When timer beeps, use natural pressure release for about 10 minutes, then release any remaining pressure.

6. Remove the steamer basket immediately and place the asparagus on a serving platter so they are no longer cooked by residual heat from the Instant Pot.

7. Serve and enjoy!

Chicken Tikka Bites

Preparation time: 2 hours 4 minutes

Cook time: 5 minutes

Total time: 2 hours 9 minutes

Serves: 2

Ingredients:

- 1 Chicken Breast
- 1 Tbsp. Greek Yoghurt
- ½ Lemon juice and rind
- 1 Tsp. Ginger Puree
- 1 Tsp. Garlic Puree
- 1 Tsp. Chili Powder
- 1 Tsp. Coriander
- 1 Tsp. Cumin
- 1 Tsp. Mixed Spice
- 1 Tsp. Turmeric
- 1 Tsp. Garam Masala
- 1 Tsp. Masala Powder
- Salt & Pepper

Cooking Instructions:

1. Place a large strip of silver foil onto your worktop. Add all your seasonings to it.

2. Place the chicken breast on top and season it well with salt and pepper. Drizzle with your lemon juice and add your Greek yoghurt.

3. Seal it and then give it a good bash with a rolling pin on the side that has the seasoning as this will spread the flavoring.

4. Place it in the fridge for a couple of hours to marinate. Put 200ml of water into the bottom of your Instant Pot, add your steaming shelf and place the silver foil packet on top.

5. Secure the lid making sure steam release valve is in the proper sealed position. Select Manual High Pressure to cook for 4 minutes.

6. When timer beeps, use natural pressure release for about 10 minutes, then release any remaining pressure. Serve and enjoy!

Cheddar Bacon Ale Dip

Preparation time: 10 minutes

Cook time: 10 minutes

Total time: 20 minutes

Serves: 4 cups

Ingredients:

- 18 Oz. cream cheese, softened
- ¼ Cup of sour cream
- 1 Tbsp. Dijon mustard
- 1 Tsp. garlic powder
- 1 Cup of beer or nonalcoholic beer
- 1 Lb. bacon strips, cooked and crumbled
- 2 Cups of shredded cheddar cheese
- ¼ Cup of heavy whipping cream
- 1 Green onion, thinly sliced
- Soft pretzel bites

Cooking Instructions:

1. In a greased Instant Pot, combine cream cheese, sour cream, mustard and garlic powder until smooth.

2. Stir in beer; add bacon, reserving 2 tbsp. Secure the lid making sure steam release valve is in the proper sealed position.

3. Select Manual High Pressure to cook for 6 minutes. When timer beeps, use natural pressure release for about 10 minutes, then release any remaining pressure.

4. Select sauté setting, and adjust for normal heat. Stir in cheese and heavy cream. Cook and stir for about 4 minutes or until mixture has thickened.

5. Transfer to serving dish. Sprinkle with onion, reserved bacon and also with pretzel bun bites.

6. Serve and enjoy!

Hoisin Meatballs

Preparation time: 15 minutes

Cook time: 10 minutes

Total time: 25 minutes

Serves: 5

Ingredients:

- 1 Cup of dry red wine or beef broth
- 1 Tbsp. hoisin sauce
- 1 Tbsp. soy sauce
- 1 Large egg, lightly beaten
- Green onions, chopped
- ¼ Cup of finely chopped onion
- ¼ Cup of minced fresh cilantro
- 2 Garlic cloves, minced
- ½ Tsp. salt
- ½ Tsp. pepper
- 1 Lb. ground beef
- 1 Lb. ground pork
- Sesame seeds

Cooking Instructions:

1. Whisk together wine, hoisin sauce and soy sauce in your Instant Pot. Boil and reduce heat; simmer until liquid is reduced slightly.

2. In a large bowl, combine next seven ingredients. Add beef and pork; mix lightly but thoroughly. Shape into 1" meatballs. Put the mixture into Instant Pot.

3. Secure the lid making sure steam release valve is in the proper sealed position.

4. Select Manual High Pressure to cook for 10 minutes.

5. When timer beeps, use natural pressure release for about 10 minutes, then release any remaining pressure.

6. Sprinkle with sesame seeds.

7. Serve and enjoy!

Hearty Pork & Black Bean Nachos

Preparation time: 15 minutes

Cook time: 38 minutes

Total time: 53 minutes

Serves: 5

Ingredients:

- 1 Package (4 oz.) beef jerky
- 25 Lb. pork spareribs, cut into 2-rib sections
- 2 Cans (15 oz. each) black beans, rinsed and drained
- 1 Cup of chopped onion
- Bacon strips, cooked and crumbled
- 1 Tsp. minced garlic
- 1 Tsp. crushed red pepper flakes
- 2 Cups of beef broth, divided
- Tortilla chips

Optional toppings: shredded cheddar cheese, sour cream, thinly sliced green onions, pickled jalapeno slices and chopped tomatoes

Cooking Instructions:

1. Pulse beef jerky in a food processor until finely ground.

2. Working in batches, place 1 pound ribs in your Instant Pot; top with half the jerky, two cans beans, ½ cup of onion, three bacon strips, 2 tsp. garlic and ½ tsp. red pepper flakes.

3. Pour in 2 cups of broth. Lock lid; make sure vent is closed. Select Manual High Pressure to cook for 40 minutes.

4. When timer beeps, use natural pressure release for about 10 minutes, then release any remaining pressure.

5. Select manual setting; adjust pressure to high and set time for 40 minutes.

6. Remove from Instant Pot; make second batch by adding remaining ingredients to the Instant Pot. Repeat previous procedure.

7. When cool enough to handle, remove meat from bones; discard bones. Shred meat with two forks.

8 Select sauté setting and adjust for high heat; heat through. Strain pork mixture. Turn onto serving plates with chips and toppings as desired.

9 Serve and enjoy!

INSTANT POT DESSERT RECIPES

Blueberry Cornmeal Breakfast Cake

Preparation time: 10 minutes

Cook time: 45 minutes

Total time: 55 minutes

Serves: 5

Ingredients:

- 1 (8.5 oz.) Box Jiffy cornbread mix
- 1 Tbsp. ground flax seed
- 1 Tbsp. chia seeds
- 1 Egg
- ½ Cup of milk
- 1 Cup of blueberries
- 2 Tbsp. honey

Cooking Instructions:

1. Place trivet inside Instant Pot then add 1 cup of water to inner pot.

2. Grease a circular baking dish that will fit inside your Instant Pot and set aside.

3. In a medium mixing bowl, whisk together cornbread mix, flax, chia, egg, and milk then gently stir in blueberries.

4. Pour batter into prepared baking dish then carefully lower onto trivet.

5. Secure the lid making sure steam release valve is in the proper sealed position.

6. Select Manual High Pressure to cook for 35 minutes.

7. When timer beeps, use natural pressure release for about 8 minutes, then release any remaining pressure.

8. Share onto serving Plates with honey.

9. Serve and enjoy!

Apple Bread with Salted Caramel Icing

Preparation time: 15 minutes

Cook time: 1 hour 10 minutes

Total time: 1 hour 25 minutes

Serves: 8

Calories 548 kcal

Ingredients:

- 2 Cups of apples Peeled Cored, and cubed
- 1 Cup of sugar
- 4 Eggs
- 1 Tbsp. vanilla
- 1 Tbsp. apple pie spice
- 2 Cups of flour
- 1 Stick butter
- 1 Tbsp. baking powder

Topping:

- 1 Stick salted butter
- 2 Cups of brown sugar
- 1 Cup of heavy cream
- 2 Cups of powdered sugar

Cooking Instructions:

1. In your mixer cream together eggs, butter, apple pie spice, and sugar until creamy and smooth.

2. Stir in your apples. In another bowl mix flour and baking powder. Add your flour mix to your wet mixture.

3. Pour into your 7" spring form pan. Place your trivet in the bottom of your Instant pot and put one cup of water. Place your pan on the trivet.

4. Secure the lid making sure steam release valve is in the proper sealed position. Select Manual High Pressure to cook for 1 hour 10 minutes.

5. When timer beeps, use natural pressure release for about 10 minutes, then release any remaining pressure. Remove and top with Icing.

6. Serve and enjoy!

Chunky Apple Cake

Preparation time: 8 minutes

Cook time: 50 minutes

Total time: 58 minutes

Serves: 5

Ingredients:

- ¾ Cup of vanilla Greek yogurt
- ½ Cup of vegetable oil
- 1 Cup of sugar
- 1 Egg
- 1 Tsp. vanilla
- 2 Cups of peeled & chopped apples
- 2 Cups of all-purpose flour
- ½ Cup of oatmeal
- 1 Tsp. baking soda
- ½ Tsp. kosher salt
- ½ Tsp. grated nutmeg
- 1 Tsp. cinnamon
- ¼ Cup of chopped walnuts or pecans
- ¼ Cup of shredded sweetened coconut

Cooking Instructions:

1. Carefully grease heat proof container that can fit into your Instant Pot.

2. In a different bowl, whisk together yogurt, oil, sugar, egg, vanilla, and chopped apples. Stir in flour, oatmeal, baking soda, salt, nutmeg, and cinnamon until just combined, being careful not to over mix.

3. Fold in nuts and coconut then pour batter into heat-proof container. Place trivet inside Instant Pot and add 1 ½ cup of water. Place cake on top of trivet.

4. Secure the lid making sure steam release valve is in the proper sealed position. Select Manual High Pressure to cook for 30 minutes.

5. When timer beeps, use natural pressure release for about 8 minutes, then release any remaining pressure. Remove from Instant Pot, loosen edges, and flip onto serving platter.

6. Serve and enjoy!

Apple Crisp

Preparation time: 8 minutes

Cook time: 9 minutes

Total time: 17 minutes

Serves: 5

Ingredients:

- Medium sized apples, peeled and chopped into chunks
- 1 Tsp. cinnamon
- ½ Tsp. nutmeg
- ½ Cup of water
- 1 Tbsp. maple syrup
- 1 Tbsp. butter
- ¾ Cup of old fashioned rolled oats
- ¼ Cup of flour
- ¼ Cup of brown sugar
- ½ Tsp. salt

Cooking Instructions:

1. Place apples on the bottom of your Instant Pot.

2. Sprinkle with cinnamon and nutmeg. Top with water and maple syrup.

3. Melt the butter. In a small bowl, mix together melted butter, oats, flour, brown sugar and salt.

4. Secure the lid on the instant pot. Select Manual High Pressure to cook for 9 minutes.

5. When timer beeps, use natural pressure release for about 10 minutes, then release any remaining pressure.

6. Serve and enjoy!

Molten Mocha Cake

Preparation time: 8 minutes

Cook time: 20 minutes

Total time: 28 minutes

Serves: 6

Ingredients:

- 1 Cup of water
- Large Nellie's Free Range Eggs
- 1 ½ Cups of sugar
- 1/2 Cup of butter, melted
- 1 Tbsp. vanilla extract
- 1 Cup of all-purpose flour
- ½ Cup of baking cocoa
- 1 Tbsp. instant coffee granules
- ¼ Tsp. salt
- Fresh raspberries or sliced fresh strawberries and vanilla ice cream (optional)

Cooking Instructions:

1. Pour water into Instant Pot.

2. In a large bowl, beat eggs, sugar, butter and vanilla until blended. In another bowl, whisk flour, cocoa, coffee granules and salt; gradually beat into egg mixture.

3. Transfer to a greased baking dish. Cover loosely with foil to prevent moisture from getting into dish. Place on a trivet with handles; Put into Instant Pot.

4. Secure the lid on the instant pot. Select Manual High Pressure to cook for 20 minutes.

5. When timer beeps, use natural pressure release for about 10 minutes, then release any remaining pressure.

6. Serve and enjoy!

Mason Jar Steel Cut Oats

Preparation time: 7 minutes

Cook time: 20 minutes

Total time: 27 minutes

Serves: 1

Ingredients:

- ¼ Cup of steel cut oats
- 1 Tbsp. pure maple syrup
- 1 Tbsp. chia seeds
- Pinch of salt
- ½ Cup of the extras (fresh or dried fruit, nuts, coconut, spices)
- 1 Cup of hot tap water

Cooking Instructions:

1. Add oats, syrup, chia seeds, salt and the extras into a pint size mason jar. Add water, leaving 1½ inches of headspace.

2. Shake until everything is well distributed and the chia seeds are not clumping together.

3. Place a short rack in the bottom of the pot. Pour 1 cup of water into the Instant Pot. Secure the lid on the instant pot.

4. Select Manual High Pressure to cook for 20 minutes. When timer beeps, use natural pressure release for about 10 minutes, then release any remaining pressure.

5. Remove the jars from the pot and place on a cooling rack or hot pad. (Do not open the jars until contents have settled).

6. Carefully remove the lid, stir the oats and top with a dollop of frozen whipped cream and garnish.

7. Serve and enjoy!

Vanilla Cheesecake

Preparation time: 18 minutes

Cook time: 63 minutes

Total time: 1 hour 21 minutes

Serves: 6

Ingredients:

- 1 Cup of water
- ¾ Cup of graham cracker crumbs
- 1 Tbsp. plus 2/3 cup sugar, divided
- ¼ Tsp. ground cinnamon
- 2 Tbsp. butter, melted
- Packages (8 ounces each) cream cheese, softened
- 3 Tsp. vanilla extract
- 2 Large Nellie's Free Range Eggs, lightly beaten

Optional Toppings:

- 25 Oz. white baking chocolate, chopped
- 1 Tbsp. heavy whipping cream
- Sliced fresh strawberries or raspberries, optional

Cooking Instructions:

1. Pour water into Instant Pot. Mix cracker crumbs, 1 tbsp. sugar and cinnamon; stir in butter. Press onto bottom and about 1 inch up sides of prepared pan.

2. In small bowl, beat cream cheese and remaining sugar until smooth. Beat in vanilla. Add eggs; beat on low speed just until combined.

3. Cover cheesecake tightly with foil. Place spring form pan on a trivet with handles; Put into Instant Pot. Secure the lid on the instant pot.

4. Select Manual High Pressure to cook for 1 hour 3 minutes. When timer beeps, use natural pressure release for about 10 minutes, then release any remaining pressure.

5. Remove spring form pan from Instant Pot; remove foil. Cool cheesecake on a wire rack 1 hour. Loosen sides from pan with a knife. Top with melted chocolate and cream, sprinkle with berries.

6. Serve and enjoy!

www.ingramcontent.com/pod-product-compliance
Lightning Source LLC
Chambersburg PA
CBHW081748100526
44592CB00015B/2346